Divorced:
A Woman's Struggle
Through Recovery

Rosemary Barocsi

Divorced:
A Woman's Struggle
Through Recovery

Rosemary Barocsi

PUBLISHED BY:
BRENTWOOD CHRISTIAN PRESS
4000 BEALLWOOD AVENUE
COLUMBUS, GEORGIA 31904

Introduction

Every day since our twenty-year marriage ended in divorce several questions deeply troubled me. **What was his real incentive to call it quits?** We had the best years to look forward to; the last of our four children was seventeen. The reason he stated, he could not live with my faults any longer. I didn't press him for a further explanation at the time, but ever since his summation of our relationship I kept asking myself **what in the world did I do wrong?**

Vividly recalling the day the sheriff delivered the document, officially notifying me of my husband's intent, I scanned the paper and questioned the word "**Incompatible**" as it leaped off the page. How could I become incompatible after twenty years?

I wanted the security of a lasting marriage, a happy home, happy well-adjusted children, and someone to share my life with and grow old together. We both made a personal commitment to live by the convictions of our faith in God before we met so I felt confident, and assumed ours would be a lifelong marriage. Our spiritual commitment would get us through difficult times, so I naturally thought nothing could possibly separate us, we would be together "until death do us part".

My mind shot back to the time I contemplated marrying him; young trim and pretty, I was a happy person, before we met. I had no children from my previous marriage; he received custody of his four-year-old daughter and three year old son, so I became an instant mom from the very beginning of our union. Being a step mom was not as easy as I naively imagined it would be, especially after our son and daughter eventually came along. With no previous parenting experience, I strived to be a good wife and mother.

I felt rejected, thrown away, humiliated and angry. Gray haired and quite a few excess pounds added; time is unkind to a woman's body after twenty years. "He stole my youth;" I shouted deep within my heart. "Who would want me now"? I cringed as I checked "divorced" in the designated box when I had to reveal my marital status on applications, one more degrading experience having to publicly disclose the undeserved title. Society is fickle, especially toward women who are divorced, and I worried if people would prejudge and label me a loser, husband/wife stealer, and view me as easy prey for sexual favors, as descriptive words came to mind from the past. As I searched for significance, inner feelings of unity, safety, and security, were replaced by abandonment, loneliness and despair.

Several months after our divorce, I heard my ex was getting married again and another punch to my already low self-worth plummeted me into a deeper depression. Wounds of rejection became unbearably fresh all over again. An article I read years ago about the mental anguish divorced people continually go through came to mind. The majority of people interviewed concluded they would rather endure the death of a spouse than endure divorce because living with sweet memories of a departed loved one is easier to accept, than living with the constant presence of an ex partner living happily somewhere out there, with someone else. I was not able to identify with the story then, remembering, "I'm glad I don't have that to worry about." I can feel every descriptive word of emotional upheaval, the loneliness and hurt that lurk at one's door. Without a shred of doubt, loneliness and despair were constant visitors to my roller coaster emotions, holding me steadfast in their crippling grip.

Contents

Why Me Lord?

We were members of a vibrant Christian bible teaching Evangelical Free Church. It had been our place of worship for many years, and I felt comfortable with my spiritual family. After our divorce when I attended, minor blips in pastor Dave's microphone seemed to intercept meaningful statements in his sermon. "Your presence here in God's house is why pastors microphone goes haywire. "something deep within seemed to say. Believing the lie, I thought, yes, it was the sin of my divorce causing "spiritual interference" in the electronics. I began to feel alienated from God and my spiritual brothers and sisters, my mind impressed with the thought I no longer belonged. Shame shrouded my emotions. My conscience dictated I had to leave.

Hoping to find a new church home and resolve the many unanswered questions to **why** it all happened, I decided to visit the church of a pastor who counseled us several years ago. Looking for a place to sit, I starred at other families whispering to each other waiting for the service to begin. Someone from our past approached and asked about my ex. When I shared we were divorced, she took a step back and offered an apology, then suggested I attend Divorce Recovery. During the sermon, I sat quietly trying to concentrate, but condemning thoughts occupied my mind. I felt different, disconnected, as though I had some kind of plague. At the end of the service, I waited for most of the people to leave, and then shared my dreaded news with Pastor Mark as we exchanged a customary handshake. I could plainly see tears in his eyes as I stammered out the words. His response validated my pain. I wept driving home, feeling sorry for myself. I did not fit in anywhere. I heard myself saying God hates divorce. Convinced I was unacceptable to God, I surmised the "why" question would not have a spiritual answer. I believed that lie, too. Emotional wounds dampened my desire to continue attending church, Sunday mornings I watched TV evangelists to fill the need for spiritual guidance, and frequently asked God to fix my broken heart.

As fall and winter approached, happy memories of cooking and baking, and decorating our home for the holidays ceased to be a reality. The anticipation of joyful times became dreaded, painful reminders that we were no longer a family unit sharing a special time together. Everyday life turned out that way, too. I felt terrible as I watched my grown son and daughter try to adjust. They were good at hiding their feelings but eventually the wake of sadness swept through their lives as they began to process their own brokenness.

Following the advice of the person several months previous, I signed up for Divorce Recovery, an eight- week workshop offered by another church in the area, to help people through the grieving process of divorce. I attended two classes, felt out of place and quit. My ex and I agreed to a monetary settlement from the sale of our home, which gave a false sense of security. I thought all I really needed was enough money to handle whatever came my way.

Time was supposed to heal all wounds but my brain churned every waking moment and even in my dreams. Thoughts uncontrollably shot back and forth like a boomerang, one moment consumed with negative input that fed fear to my heart, then, reeled to sweet memories of joyful moments peacefully worshipping God in church. The longer I stayed away from church the stronger estrangement grew. I could not live without God in my life. I prayed, pleading for His acceptance then contemplated attending; motivated to prove my ex had no "spiritual" grounds to end our marriage, resolved to search for the answers **I wanted;** that I did not contribute to the breakdown of our relationship. I was a faithful hard working wife and mother committed to uphold our vows until "death do us part". The decision to call it quits was not mine, and I vowed to prove my innocence to his charge of "Incompatibility", no matter how long it took. If only there were a Sunday school class for people in my situation, but I believed that possibility could never be.

My heart relentlessly hungered for a spiritual home to meet with God. I decided to end futile attempts to try to find answers through my own strength and turn to God to heal the growing intense feeling of rejection. A very close friend suggested church to be my only true answer. Her counsel startled then prompted me to think about attending, but fear and anxiety blocked me from transferring thoughts into action, yet I could not dismiss her optimistic words. Consumed with hope and fear, my mind became a battlefield where good and evil dueled until an affirmative decision resulted. Relief blanketed my thoughts. When Sunday morning came, fear and anxiety attempted to discourage me again but I stuck to my decision, fought the negative emotional attack and forced myself to attend church.

That very Sunday Pastor Dave announced a new bible class for women who were hurting from spiritual and emotional pain. Tears welled in my eyes and I sat, immersed in total amazement. I whispered, "Could you have heard my desperate cry, God?" A peaceful awareness enveloped my spirit dispelling the loneliness and despair that once had a stranglehold of me. Tears flowed as I sat, feeling God's unconditional love filling every fiber of my being and somehow I felt I was not alone any longer.

I attended the new class the following week, and, the next, and the next. We studied God's Word and another book written by Dr. Charles Stanley, "**The Source of My Strength**" **Dr. Stanley** revealed a candid transparent view into his life and how he discovered painful childhood experiences hindered his spiritual growth in certain areas of his life. The concept for some reason seemed to take hold of me. As we studied, we learned truth from the bible and replaced lies we believed about ourselves.

Barbara, our group leader, suggested we start a journal to record our discoveries and spiritual growth. Remembering the encouragement I received from my ex-mother-in-law about the letters I wrote to her full of fascinating and sometimes funny life experiences raising her grandchildren and the happenings around our home sparked an interest in pursuing Barb's suggestion, besides, I loved to write.

An Invitation

My life is very much like the average person; yet unresolved hurtful incidents greatly influenced the choices I made and I traveled an emotional road riddled with potholes I kept falling in. Recalling pleasant as well as unpleasant memories, I believe, was the most significant step to my healing process, because that is where I discovered the roots to the when and why of hurtful incidents that injured my spirit and stunted my emotional maturation. Reediting each of what I thought was my last copy, permitted me to dig a little deeper into gray areas where I drew wrong conclusions to the "stormy times" in my life. Pull up a chair alongside and enter the past with me. I begin my journey where I replaced church attendance with watching TV evangelists on Sunday mornings.

Pushing the Past Aside

Striving to find answers, I had nothing but time to think about life changing decisions I made in the past, for one; marrying my **first** husband for all the wrong reasons, then initiating our divorce because I could not make him stop drinking. Twenty-some-years later I found myself painfully reaping the consequences of a **second** hasty marriage trying to fix the mistakes of my past, and experiencing the sting of what it feels like to be on the receptive end of broken marriage vows.

After our home in the country sold, my son Dana and I moved into a little two-bedroom brick apartment in a nearby town closer to the convalescent hospital where I worked at the time. Our new abode was emotionally comforting, for some reason it felt like "home" to me. Later, when writing about my childhood, I recalled pleasant memories of the government housing project and the red brick house our family occupied so many years ago.

Several months passed and somehow I pushed aside feelings of rejection and anger and fearfully accepted my single status. I reasoned I was healthy, had plenty of money, a good job, and could come and go as I pleased. I had no responsibilities, and no one to answer to, except God.

I concentrated on my new career and on days off, shopped and bought little trinkets to decorate our tiny apartment. Shopping became an escape to avoid angry feelings that festered in my heart. **To stay connected with God, I prayed silently to myself, which I thought kept me in communication, but it was usually a one-way conversation, me to God; I wasn't listening to the still small Voice that prompted me as I went about my daily activities.**

Browsing through a discount store one day and silently talking to God, I was proud to inform Him I had gotten over the pain of my husband leaving, thinking I was ready to accept the truth of why my

11

marriage failed. I knew God spoke to people's hearts through reading the bible, and hoped He would somehow enlighten me. When I chose to read my bible, I twisted the words and projected all blame on my ex. I did not realize I had to focus God's Word of correction to my life, to see where I needed to examine my own behavior and attitude, areas where I needed to change. **God put my answer on hold for six years, because the prideful condition of my heart blocked me from accepting any truth from His Word at that time.**

Dana found odd jobs at a nearby marina and at dinner, he shared stories about his adventures. One evening he came home very excited and exclaimed he had a once in a lifetime opportunity to obtain a free boat; all he needed to do was repair and make it seaworthy. After informing the owner of the marina of his interest in salvaging it, he became the proud owner of a thirty-eight foot wooden boat, badly needing major repairs to the inside as well as outside of it. A fellow he met helped repair the huge vessel. I made curtains; seat cushion covers and helped scrape off the old paint from the upper deck. Working alongside my son and his friends kept me busy; I didn't have time to think about problems. My weight dropped and I began to feel good about myself again. After months of labor, it was ready for launching. My son hired the crane operator at the marina to move it to the water. We watched with excited anticipation as the crane lifted and moved the humongous thirty-eight foot vessel. The gigantic boat grunted and groaned as it was lifted off the sand, carefully carried in-between a huge two story u shaped machine with nylon straps that cradled and hugged the vessel tightly, transferring it to its new home in the water. The boat settled to the "safe water level" line my son painted around the sides, and began swaying simultaneously to the waves in the water. Dana threw the mooring ropes to his friend, to secure the vessel to the dock. As the planks quickly soaked up the murky seawater, we waited to see if there were any leaks. Two hours later, we headed home. Dana awoke early the next day and eagerly headed off to check on his boat. He found it listing at the bow several inches below the water level line. Discovering a leak and faulty bilge pump, he repaired the problems. A week later, the boat still afloat, we celebrated.

Next project was to get it powered up. Dana found two almost new motors, I wrote a check to purchase them and he installed the massive machinery below deck, hooked up the gas lines and paraphernalia that were necessary to give it life and get it moving. We putted around near the shore; then ventured into deeper water and visited other marinas nearby. The captains of other wooden boats waved to us as we cruised by; some came along side and shared stories and pictures of my son's boat when it was new. Dana could not afford to restore the vessel to its original condition, but in spite of always needing work and always needing gas, he was proud of his accomplishment to refurbish it to seaworthiness.

He invited me on several excursions and a picnic across the bay. We joined families that were already there, and set up our portable bar-b-queue grill on the back of the boat. I sat watching young couples play together in the water and mourned the loss of the bond between two people in love as scenes from fun times we had filtered through my thoughts. I felt like a misfit. No matter how I tried to pull out of my depression, I ended up at a dead end. I knew I could talk to God, but I wasn't sure He was listening. **God was there all the time, patiently waiting for me to run out of ways to heal my own heart.**

Another Rejection

The morning hours passed quickly where I worked as a nurse; evenings were lonely. Emotional neediness and insecurity motivated immature behavior as I expose an incident that I would much rather have forgotten. A fellow I had not seen since grammar school entered my life shortly after my divorce. His father, admitted as a patient where I worked, needed around the clock nursing care, and he visited his dad daily. A co-worker shared that my school chum was not married. Perhaps I needed a husband to fill the emptiness in my heart. Yes, my conscience dictated, a husband is what I needed. Feeling confident with my weight loss, I conjured up a great scenario and began pursuing him. In my youth, I was pretty, enough to attract any boy. Acting on adolescent impulses I flirted, hinted, and practically threw myself at him in a desperate attempt to fix my broken life. When he didn't respond to several attempts to get his attention, I began to observe he tried more often to avoid rather than seek me out. Realizing my futile attempts were going nowhere, I gave up chasing after him. Thoughts from low self-esteem echoed, "Who do you think you are some beauty queen?" "Look at you...all used up, gray hair and fifty pounds greater than when he knew you, get real, he would never pick you to marry. Again, I heard my conscience say I couldn't even attract a person my own age, another rejection added to my "feeling worthless" list.

Three Times Blessed

I switched my work schedule to full time evenings to occupy lonely nights. A few months later, I received a notice that the health insurance premium was going to be increased. Although retirement was a distant concern, reviewing the health and retirement packets was disappointing as I discovered both were not adequate now being single. I had to find another job to meet my present and future needs. Contemplating a change was upsetting, I was afraid to quit my emotionally comfortable position. Terry, my co-worker and friend had moved to another facility, and each time we spoke, she insisted I apply there. Mulling over my options, not positively sure of the outcome if I left my comfort zone, confusion and fear gripped my spirit as I wrestled with making a decision. When I received my paycheck with the increased premium deducted, plus the added retirement deduction, the incentive to make the choice to give my two-week notice was much easier. After I finalized my resignation, nightmares invaded my dreams; I did not know what was causing such turmoil.

I applied for an evening position, interviewed and hired where my friend Terry found her employment enjoyable. The nursing home had a warm friendly atmosphere and I bonded with the patients almost immediately. The workload expected was double that of my previous job, making nursing routines stressful and difficult. I strove to keep my assigned floor in order, but as unusual occurrences increased, I experienced a tremendous amount of tension trying to meet all the needs of the patients as well as keeping track of my nurses' aides. My conscious dictated I was solely responsible for whatever went wrong and my reaction and communication to an inquiry of an incident gave the appearance of guilt, as if I allowed an incident to occur. I could not

15

humanly be everywhere at all times to make sure everyone was doing their work, and patients adequately cared for.

Stress, I discovered later, was a catalyst to resurrect emotional ingrained childhood fears and God kept stretching me to gain confidence in my abilities and to overcome a false sense of guilt.

In retrospect, I can see the why of God's plan for me to chose nursing as my occupation. Disciplines I lacked, I needed to fulfill His plan for my life, to stretch my faith, weed out weak areas and build self-esteem into my character. Satan knew my weak areas too, and used all his tricks to hold me back from maturing in faith. Spiritually, I was unaware of the battle between good and evil for control of my mind.

The vehicle I drove was getting tired and in need of a major overhaul. Dana was an excellent mechanic and I relied on him to keep my car in good working order, thankful I didn't have to worry about the expense of hiring a mechanic when it needed maintenance. His advise to trade it in while it still had resale value was a wise suggestion, so on my next weekend off he and I went shopping for a newer model. He jokingly stated I needed something sportier to fit my single life style and encouraged me to purchase a sleek looking Cadillac with a "rag top".

Thirteen months had passed since we moved into our apartment; spring was just around the corner. Carol, my real estate agent, who was also my friend phoned one day, unexpectedly, and asked if I were ready to buy a house. Feeling optimistic, I said yes, and made a date with her to go house hunting. On my day off, we looked at several she had pre-arranged to see. Each of the four homes we walked through did not "feel" right. Disappointed, I suggested we call it day and confided I had signed my lease for another year; Carol persisted, stating there was only one left to look at. We arrived at a huge colonial duplex at the end of a dead end street. Newly built, the house had tan siding; no painting needed. We walked the grounds and noted a small piece of property, not a lot of yard work; a second positive aspect. Entering the front door, I felt right at home as we walked through each room. I especially liked the huge kitchen with brand new oak cabinets, and the small half bath on the first floor was a convenience. The basement had a place for a washer, dryer and the possibility of an added room with a walk out exit. Three bedrooms and full bath occupied the third floor. I agreed to purchase it forgetting about the lease I signed. The closing date was April late afternoon. Obtaining a mortgage, and getting through the red tape of not having to pay for the year's lease I signed, only God could have orchestrated. Dana and I were exhausted moving the last piece of furniture inside late that night. After setting up our beds, we said goodnight.

Awaking to the brightness of the early morning sun radiating through the uncovered double windows of my room, I got up and looked out across the yard. A huge cheery tree was magnificently in full bloom and its widely spreading branches occupied most of my view from the window. I stood awe struck, gazing at the beautiful tree, mesmerized by its colorful display. I thought about the recent changes in my life. I felt so unworthy, I did not think to ask God for anything, yet He provided more than I could ever ask for. I could not comprehend why He continued to bless me so abundantly.

Dana and I settled into our new home. After walking the grounds, we began making plans to accommodate our cars. A deep cement culvert twenty feet from the house, bordered the side of my property, the land gradually sloped downward to the culvert edge. Dana measured for a double car driveway. I ordered railroad ties and two truckloads of gravel to complete the job and was thankful to have his help with the heavy work. He took advantage of the extra space in the driveway and worked on his friends' cars.

As I attempted to plow through life on my own, God continued to confirm His presence in many ways.

Two New Companions

Dana worked with another person who had adopted a stray dog, a Doberman Pinscher. Having a variety of pets throughout his childhood, he enjoyed playing with his friend's dog each day. When he came home from work he tried to convince me to buy one for "us." The dog would be good protection he reasoned. I responded "maybe;" repeating the breed of the dog to myself, thinking, I did not like the sound of the breed, let alone having one for a pet. Story after story he told of the dog at the dock, how gentle and protective the animal was. One evening Dana came home visibly upset. His facial color was pale and his eyes reddened, I guessed from crying. He sat down on the sofa and could hardly contain his tears, stating the dog had slipped from the dock into the water and landed squarely on a wooden stake sticking up just below the surface of the water puncturing its lung. My son rushed the animal to the pet emergency hospital but the veterinarian could not save the dog. My heart broke for the animal and for my son having to go through such a terrible ordeal. **Emotionally driven** to fix his wounded spirit; I gave in, but stated that I would only consider a puppy. The next day we looked in the Yellow Pages for kennels that bred Doberman Pinschers. Pursuing kennels was futile so we phoned canine trainers, calling several until we found one. We requested a female.

A few weeks later, the dog trainer delivered our little shorthaired bundle of joy. She was six weeks old, had distinct tan and black Doberman markings, a long pointy nose, a stub for a tail, big feet, an indication, I was informed, that she was not going to stay little. Two thickly padded sticks stuck out of each of her ears held in place by white tape. He gave us legal papers and specific instructions on how to feed her and care for her ears. I hired him to teach our puppy to be obedient to both of us. We chose the name Duchess because she came from a bloodline of "Dukes", Princes' and "Ladies", but her name should have been Shadow; she was always just one step behind, I frequently tripped over her when I turned around. She loved to ride in the car and nuzzle her nose under my arm. As a pup, she strutted around the house poking her long straight nose into everything, often getting into mischief. Calling from work one day to check on our puppy, my son accessed the room monitor we had as an added feature to our answer machine and he said it sounded like we had a crew of carpenters in our house. When he arrived home, he found she had chewed a hole in the kitchen floor. She managed to find a tiny tear in the linoleum and worked on it until there was a three-foot round hole in the center. He phoned and described her delinquent behavior. I did not believe she was capable of getting into that much trouble but when I saw the damage, I remembered not securing her in the kennel before leaving for work, then proceeded to scold her. She didn't understand my scolding her so long after the fact and looked up at me tilting her head to the side. When I looked into her big brown eyes, my heart melted. We put up a six-foot stockade fence for her to freely run around the back and side yard to expend her penned up energy.

A year later, we decided to purchase another Doberman. At that time, the only dog available was Shilo, a year old female previously owned by a college age fellow who, the attendant said could not care for her. Shilo's temperament was puzzling, she didn't budge from the back seat when Dana made a pit stop, and she stood statue like, all the way home. Our vet discovered she had a bladder infection and when she was treated, a fierce loyalty and devotion to my son replaced her difficult behavior; relieved of the pain she must have experienced for so long.

My son sold his boat and bought a tiny used travel trailer to go camping. After his first campout he wanted one he could live in and invited me to a travel trailer exposition a few towns away. Each unit we entered was nicer than the previous one. I reminisced of the fun our family had years ago when we camped and reasoned my son and I could enjoy camping life. He traded in his camper as down payment and I signed to purchase a new twenty-eight foot trailer equipped with a stereo system throughout, microwave in the fully equipped kitchen; living room, bedroom, and shower.

Living at the end of a dead end street was advantageous. My driveway was long enough to accommodate the trailer as Dana backed it in. Parked along the side of my home, it was out of sight and my neighbors didn't complain. He hooked up to the electricity and shared my phone line enjoying the comforts of his trailer home.

Late summer, trailer in tow and the two dogs corralled in the back of his pick up, Dana and I headed toward a campsite near Lake George. The scenery was beautiful as we traveled. Memories of our family vacations drifted through my thoughts again, occupying time as we drove. We arrived at our destination six hours later, checked in , found our site and Dana detached the trailer and connected the utilities while I fed and watered the dogs. After settling them in, we hopped in his truck and rode around looking for things to do. I signed us up for a two-hour dinner cruise around Lake George. We stopped in a few places that looked interesting, then returned to freshen up, change clothes, and replenished food and water for our puppies. When all was secure, we headed off to the marina and our dinner date on board ship.

The dining quarters were below deck and the waiter escorted us to our table. We chitchatted about small stuff while we ate. After dinner, we ventured to the upper deck to view the scenery. It was a beautiful evening and the cool air felt refreshing as we sailed up the lake. My son left me briefly to explore more of the ship and I stayed put near the upper guardrail. Old mansions along the shore became more interesting as I read of their history in one of the pamphlets I picked up. Eventually my eyes gravitated to couples as they stood arm in arm, and my heart began to ache again. An overwhelming feeling of loneliness came over me and I stood trying to stop the tears as they unceasingly flowed from my eyes. My son returned and without saying a word, he put his arm around me. I buried my face in his shoulder and sobbed. I felt so detached from the world. I managed to mask my grieving heart for the rest of the evening but I cried myself to sleep that night.

After breakfast, I cleaned the camper, and Dana went bike riding. I walked the dogs for exercise and explored the campground a little each day. Lake George was further north, the late summer seasonal change in the leaves were starting to change color, flowers lining some of the sidewalks were profusely arrayed in early fall colors of gold, red, orange and yellow. As my puppies and I strolled along the pathways I daydreamed pleasant memories of yesteryear, places we camped, attractions we visited. I loved the crispness of color and the coolness of the weather change in autumn; my ex and I took our honeymoon in the fall. One of the dogs spotted a squirrel and jerked on the leash as she tried to break away. Mustering strength to gain control of an eighty pound "puppy" instantly brought all my senses to immediate attention and jolted my mind back to the present. We finished our walk and I replenished water for the dogs. Depression visited again, why couldn't I fill this hole in my heart.

Our return trip was uneventful and the dogs pranced with excitement seeing the familiar site of our home. I just wanted to crawl into a little hole and live out the rest of my life there.

I battled with depression. My thoughts were constantly at work trying to resolve the spiraling intensity of feeling abandoned. Emotional exhaustion eroded my heart. My worse fear was spending the rest of my life alone, forever, with no one to take care of me.

A Happy Reunion

God saw the desperation of my heart, and brought my daughter back into my life. She was twenty-two. We had not spoken since the divorce. I believed something I said hurt her and was silently suffering the guilt of losing her as well as her father. She met her future husband at work and was busily involved with him and his family. He had a close, loving relationship with his parents, especially his dad, who was gravely ill with cancer. My daughter drove his father to doctor appointments several times a week. His dad lost his battle with cancer. As several months passed, he missed those precious moments with his dad and encouraged my daughter to call and renew our relationship. She struggled with mixed emotions as she avoided his initial suggestion to contact me. Through his persistence, she phoned. Our first conversation initiated confusion in my mind as I emotionally clung to the parent/child bond from years gone by. She had been on her own so long, it was difficult trying to bridge the gap of the silent years we lost contact, and I struggled to understand the person she had become, but still overjoyed to hear her voice and cried after we hung up. We visited often. Ever since she was little there was never a time she'd be at a loss for words and confided many of her activities with me barring no restraints on events she lived through previously, including her present condition, she thought she was pregnant; and while visiting me did a home pregnancy test that revealed positive results. Seven months later my precious little granddaughter was born. Thirteen months later, my second precious granddaughter blessed our family. I offered to share my home; fearful for her and my grandchildren's safety living in the area she could afford. My son and I finished off the basement into a little apartment and my daughter moved in the main living quarters.

Dana was happy sleeping in his trailer in the driveway, my daughter and grandkids lived above me. Alone no longer, everyone I loved was close by.

A few months later,my daughter moved to Florida rather abruptly. For weeks I wandered through the empty rooms reminiscing happy times with her and my beautiful granddaughters. Not hearing from her, I moved back upstairs.

I kept busy with unfinished outdoor projects, and ordered a truckload of dirt to fill in a deep gap at the end of the patio first. I learned how to do many things working along side of my ex, and felt confident I could accomplish the tasks I planned. I was not present when he ordered material so I did not know I had to specify the composition of dirt when I placed my order. The first shovel was heavy, full of clay and I realized my mistake too late. Each day I moved a few wheelbarrows of the dirt to the side- yard. The weather was in my favor for a few days, but eventually a forecasted rainstorm moved slowly overhead. I managed to reduce the mound of dirt to a couple of wheelbarrows. As the rain gently fell, I started thinking how easy it was for the two of us working to move mountains of dirt together and got agitated no one was around to help. The rain grew more intense. I worked feverishly to finish, my foot slipped off the tool, I lost my balance and fell knee deep in the hole I was trying to fill. The clouds burst forth a torrential down pour. Sopping wet, I sunk to my knees and cried as I tossed the shovel aside. The adrenaline rush from increasing emotional anguish got me out of the hole and into the house where I soothed feelings of frustration with food, my thoughts flooded with questions. What did I do? Where did I fail?

God seemed to hear each of my heart's desperate cries. My daughter called and asked if my home was still available. I cried, welcomed her and moved back downstairs; thankful I would not be alone any longer.

My grown progeny had occasional conflicts living so close together. I attempted to be the peacemaker, unsuccessful at any attempt to solve their disputes. When my son announced he was moving to Florida, I thought I would never see him again. He was always there for me, what would I do without him? Who would fix things in the house? Who would rescue me when I had car trouble? At first I felt he was abandoning me too, but I also knew deep down in my heart I had to let him go, he was twenty-four years old but I was emotionally dependent on him.

As weeks passed after my sons' departure, I focused my attention to outside yard work and ordered material to complete landscaping projects. We worked on spreading the gravel after the rotting railroad ties were removed, to even out the sloping landscape, then added an additional three feet of cement block building the height of the inside wall of the culvert to the level of the foundation of my home. At night, my daughter and I would talk after the children went to bed. As we exchanged painful memories, false emotional guilt began twisting my thoughts from hurtful incidents I believed were entirely my fault; circumstances that were, in reality, beyond my control. I made unnecessary purchases to make my home more comfortable and promised things I was not financially capable to freely give.

My nest egg dwindled little by little. Credit card debt, mortgage, utilities, insurances escalated. Payments I agreed to be responsible for strained my shrinking paycheck, threatening my financial security. My mind whirled in confusion as I continued on the financial suicidal course, grossly over spending. Working overtime to replenish what I spent was not a favorable option. Being older, I did not have the stamina to embrace that choice. **The settlement from our divorce did not provide the well being I imagined.** Extreme anxiety from the uncertainty of my future caused fear and stress to control my conversation. Frustrated, I tried to convey my financial dilemma in a loving way, but harsh words spilled out instead, causing misunderstanding and hurt feelings.

Several months later, my daughter and er husband purchased a home of their own and moved a mile away. Being close to financial ruin, and feeling rejected again, I crumpled lower in despair not knowing where to find relief. I felt desperately alone. Betrayed by my ex and abandoned by my children, I prayed to God to take me home. When He didn't, I felt God had left me too. I heard my conscience say once more, no one cared, not even God.

I learned much later that the intensity of rejection I felt at the time was not actually when the seed of rejection was planted in my life. It actually imprisoned my emotions many years ago and revisited repeatedly throughout my life.

The "Proverbial Fork in the Road"

My home became painfully quiet. I spent hours thinking about all the yesterdays of my life. I walked away from my first marriage. At the end of my second marriage, I was now experiencing what total rejection really feels like, even my own children did not want to live with me. Alone and afraid of what the future held in store, I had reached my proverbial fork in the road at the age of fifty-two. Having money, keeping busy; what the world offered did not satisfy my deep longing to feel loved, and accepted. I was ready and willing to do anything that would take away the intense pain from feeling rejected and abandoned. I needed help to move on with my life. I dared to approach God again and asked…"Why, Lord?"

In the next heartbeat, my thoughts shifted to church, to good times when my spirit felt at peace singing and talking to God. A deep longing for God stirred within my soul. At that moment, a compelling urge spurred me to call someone I had not spoken to in a very long time. *(Thank you God.)* I phoned Dottie, a dear friend I spiritually bonded with when I became a new believer. I was happy to hear her voice when she answered. We chatted, updating each other with family news, I began to cry. As the sensitive person she had been, she invited me to have lunch with her on Saturday.

I wept as we hugged; it was good to see her again. I poured out my disappointments. When I confessed that I had not been attending church, she advised me to go and seek God for answers. I said I would but in my heart at that moment, I really did not mean it. She said she was going to call me Sunday morning, and I knew she would. I laid awake that evening thinking about her advice to go to church. Nothing there for me, I thought, probably the same old Sunday school classes; certainly not a class for hurting or divorced women.

The following day I awoke to the urgent still small voice of the Holy Spirit prodding me to get out of bed. Resisting the effort to get up, a spiritual battle began to take place in my head. After what seemed to be an hour or so, I thought if I had time to shower and dress, I would get up. I glanced at my clock, hoping to have procrastinated the time away. Focusing my eyes on the hands, it read seven thirty, plenty of time to get ready with a few moments to spare. A positive feeling clicked in my spirit at that moment and I dismissed the urge to roll over and pull the blanket over my head. I dragged my body out of bed. An overwhelming feeling of fear struck the minute my feet hit the floor, I felt weak, sick to my stomach, and a headache seemed to come from nowhere as I prepared to take a shower, but, sick or not, I wanted to put an end to the emotional pain I couldn't escape from. The phone rang; it was Dottie. I told her I was up and getting ready for church. Sensing something good was going to happen I truly felt different that morning getting dressed. Determined to go forward I fought the excuses of why I should stay home as they freely flowed from my thoughts driving to church encouraged by this positive feeling; nothing was going to stop me.

No Longer Alone

God's Spirit was actively preparing my heart to see "church" with a renewed perspective. As I entered the sanctuary, the atmosphere was inviting, people were dressed casually and they seemed more relaxed. I slipped into one of the seats in the back row. Many of the old familiar details of the worship service were changed; vastly different from the way I remembered them to be. The sea of new faces that I gazed upon as I scanned the congregation was encouraging. They emanated warmth and friendliness and as I listened to various conversations, I thought I heard the word divorce, more than once. The great singing from the congregation, the choirs had grown and all that I remembered of the musical portion of the service was still the same sweet sounds. The hand bell choir was delightful to hear and the teens did a great job playing them. God often spoke to my heart through the hymns we sang, and wouldn't you know it? Each song drew my spirit closer to Him. I loved all the music. As we stood, joy radiated from people as we sang a few old familiar choruses. People lifted their hands while they gently swayed to the rhythm of the music. Observing tears on some of the peoples' cheeks as they closed their eyes and sang filled my heart to overflowing, and I wept. It felt good to be "home" again. God was evident that day, touching each sensitive area of my heart encouraging me to continue pursuing the direction I had chosen. The ailments I experienced before coming to church vanished as I soaked in God's presence.

Our church had definitely grown. Glancing at the bulletin, I noted several small group studies added to the Sunday school hour for people seeking a recovery program. I thought about the pain and unanswered questions in my heart, and listened carefully during the announcements for any bible classes that would help relieve my inner turmoil. That particular Sunday our Pastor announced a new Adult Bible Fellowship class to women hurting from painful experiences, which included divorce, to begin the following week. I cried as I sat there stunned at what I had just heard. Overwhelmed how awesome God answered my hearts plea for help, I thought about the encouragement my good friend offered, the urgent feeling to get out of bed, get to church, and the announcement of the new class, on that particular Sunday. How truly blessed I am to have such a mighty God who sees my hurt, meets my needs and answers at just the right moment in time. I felt truly blessed to be one of His very own, and proud to be a member of the greatest Evangelical Free church on the Northeast coast.

The following Sunday was a bright beautiful day. I wondered as I showered who would be attending the class, and what subjects we would study. I started feeling sick again but ignored the symptoms, quickly dressed, jumped in my car and headed off toward a new beginning. Driving to church, I sensed a positive affirmation to the decision I made.

I thought more about the class than listening to the message. My heart raced in anticipation of the first meeting as we sang the closing hymn. Pastor Dave welcomed me at the door with a warm smile as we shook hands, and asked how I was getting along. I thanked him for asking, confided that I was anxious to join the new class for hurting women and rushed off up the stairs.

An Unexpected Surprise

Approaching the Pastor's office where the class was to meet each week, I became apprehensive. Facing people one on one after the five years I had been absent from church was going to be difficult. I hesitated for a moment then thought, "This is a new beginning for me" and mustered the courage to open the door. I walked into the room and noted a few familiar faces, surprised to see Barbara and doubly surprised to find out she was going to teach the class. She sang in the choir and was church secretary for years, so what was she doing teaching a class on divorce I thought? I remembered a brief moment several years ago when we passed each other in church. I sensed some kind of connection as I glanced into her eyes. I didn't understand that feeling then, but as Barbara grasped my hand, smiled, and welcomed me, my facial expression must have provoked her to respond by stating that she had been divorced for a couple of years. We exchanged familiarities before the class began. As more women entered the room, we introduced ourselves to each other, chatted for a few moments, and then began our class. I thought momentarily, as I gazed at the women in the room, there was every age group represented guessing the youngest in her twenties, to the oldest who confessed was in her sixties, yet we all had numerous painful experiences that weighed heavily on our hearts. We started out with prayer for God to bless our study and efforts to heal our wounded spirit. The atmosphere in the room grew warm and friendly and everyone seemed comfortable being there. Each of us shared a small portion of our lives and I realized that I was not alone, walking around with a wounded heart, feeling isolated from the "church" and the rest of the world. We were all hurting in different ways from spiritual and emotional pain.

Barbara shared her testimony with us. Her husband and she had been very active in different capacities of our church. She sang in the choir and he served as a deacon in past years. Never suspecting infidelity, she confided to not seeing the telltale signs of a wayward husband and in the beginning had no reason to doubt excuses he gave being absent from their family. Continuing on, she told us when she came to realize that their marriage of twenty-seven years was falling apart, initially, she blamed herself, then did everything she could in her own strength to keep it intact. She became fearful of people finding out and contemplated what they would think; she said running away was the logical solution. She dropped out of church separating herself from people she grew up with and loved thinking she had to protect God's honor and didn't want to disgrace His name or the church. For two years she visited other congregations to stay connected with God. As time passed, she realized that running away was not the answer. When she learned of her husband's continued behavior she found a Christian counseling center in a nearby town, and sought relief from the deep wounds of her heart. She explained that she had invited Christ into her heart as a child and being raised in a Christian home, felt more comfortable getting spiritual help for her troubled marriage. Our pastor also counseled her as she went through a very painful process. She followed every rule of our church trying to keep her marriage from ending. "Divorce wasn't supposed to happen in a Christian marriage," she stated, yet it happened. One of the board members in our congregation whom she had known for many years observed the painful process she endured and shared three very important words with her. He explained if she followed their meaning as he often did when he encountered a problem, she too, would have the strength to overcome adversity and come through any crisis victoriously. She shared them with us and stated they are the three words we absolutely needed to get us through any difficult situation. They were FIRM, FIXED and FOCUSED. She explained; if we keep our mind and heart **firmly fixed** and **focused** on Jesus, we could get through anything.

God also used the traumatic experience she went through to alert our church leaders of a vital ministry needed to come alongside the growing number of women in our congregation who are silently hurting from emotional and spiritual pain. Pastor asked if she would give her testimony at both services and she said yes, not because he asked her to, but because she believed, it was what God wanted her to do. She had great compassion for our group of ladies, and shed tears when she shared about never losing sensitivity to the pain she experienced in her past. Her words touched me, giving yet another confirmation of being exactly where God wanted me to be at that time.

She confided giving her testimony in front of the people she knew was the hardest thing she had ever done aside from her divorce, but after she finished and the service ended she was overwhelmed with the responses she received from women in pain. It became obvious that our church needed to provide a place for hurting women to meet together to learn Biblical truth to heal their wounded spirit. Our class, "Crossroads," was the result of a precious, sensitive woman being obedient to God, and willing to share her deepest hurt in front of hundreds of people. Our class includes women who are spiritually and emotionally hurting, silently suffering from low self-esteem from difficult relationships, and troubled marriages. The curriculum was easy to understand and Barbara did not set a time limit to each lesson. We progressed at a slow pace, each woman was encouraged to participate, but didn't have to if it were too uncomfortable. As each shared, the more reluctant women began to open up and expose their innermost pain. Blessed with God given wisdom, Barbara unselfishly gave us as much time as we needed to express our hurts and frustrations. We prayed for each other in class, anxious to meet together again. As we shared, confronted and conquered our spiritual battles, we learned from each other. Barbara read from scripture to validate each lesson. Learning truth from the bible gave us a clear understanding of our relationship to God in Christ. New insights gave a renewed desire to live. Learning to process the pain suffered in our past gave each of us new freedom in our spirits. Peaceful expressions replaced drawn worried looks as we shed the negative "baggage" of guilt, hurt feelings, anger and so much more. Women in difficult relationships and troubled marriages renewed their commitment to keep their marriages intact. I was inspired to greet newcomers to our class with the phrase "you are adopted" connecting each new person to the special bond we shared in that first class. We held each other up in prayer, giving us an inner strength to face whatever came our way.

Undeniable Truth

Our first study was from Charles Stanley's book *"The Source of My Strength."*[1] Dr. Stanley wrote about several unpleasant memories from his childhood that still bothered him as an adult. Until he processed those hurtful incidents, he was unable to rationally understand and spiritually grow in the areas where his spirit was injured. I skimmed the pages encouraged by his honesty and candid writing style as he revealed his private life.

Barbara gave us handouts of two trees; one, an illustration of a bitter fruit tree with negative words describing unhealthy negative reactions, and the other a healthy tree with positive words describing healthy "fruit of the Spirit" responses. I glanced at the list of words on the healthy tree then carefully studied the list on the bitter fruit tree. My agenda was to prove my innocence to the charge of incompatibility my ex labeled me with, zeroing in on the word "rejection", which I identified with. Aha! I had something to work with. Once I got past the first word, I found myself identifying with other words that described *my* behavior. There was no way I could deny any, they were all there in black and white. I wondered, Jesus was supposed to have wiped clean the sins from my past when I asked Him into my heart," I thought. He took away all the bad stuff, didn't He?

Blinded by the lie Satan planted in my thoughts that God gave me all the right answers after I became a Christian especially when I mistakenly thought the other person lacked spiritual awareness; I excused emotional outbursts of immature behavior displayed in times of extreme anxiety. I learned that denial and excuses are tools Satan uses on us to reject anyone else's opinions and decisions. I faced the truth and saw that I blamed other people when *I* made poor decisions. Emotional immaturity bound me to my "little girl years" where it all began. I later discovered the unprocessed childhood emotional traumas that motivated my adult reactions. When I confronted truth, The Holy Spirit revealed many other incidents where I caused pain in someone else's life. I began to replace mistaken truth with the truth in God's Word.

A suggestion Dr. Stanley wrote drew my attention. We were encouraged to try to remember incidents that hurt us emotionally in our childhood. That would be a good place to begin searching for answers to why I had so much bitter fruit on "my tree".

I tried to recall specific hurtful experiences driving home from church, drawing blanks. All that came to mind was the fun I had. What was so bad about my life? Insignificant incidents came to mind as weeks passed. Smidgeons of painful incidents tried to break through. A state of confusion began to block memories and feelings of anxiety rendered the mental search futile. I brushed it aside. A few days passed and I thought about my childhood again determined to remember more as I persevered, mentally trying to access file cards of past memories etched in my brain.

We were well into our study when another church in the area started their annual eight-week seminar on Divorce Recovery, a "workshop" to teach people how to get through the pain of divorce. Barbara had taken the course and encouraged everyone to attend. Thoughts of the class I attended many years ago ran through my mind and my immediate response was to say I didn't need that kind of help, then decided perhaps this time around would be different, maybe there was something I didn't grasp the first time.

Working full-time evenings as a nurse and the unusual evenings I had off prevented me from having much of a social life; every other Tuesday, every other Thursday and two weekends a month. I was somewhat surprised but happy when I read that the class met on Tuesday evenings. I would be able to attend every other week, thinking of the impossibility of getting the alternate Tuesdays off but God provided the way, and I received the time off! I smiled and said thank you to God, then to the person who gave permission at work for my request. I signed up and happily attended all the classes.

The material covered in the Divorce Recovery Workshop validated and reinforced what I had learned so far at church. Each step clearly revealed God's unique plan to heal my damaged emotions. Several instructors at divorce recovery took turns presenting various topics. One evening in particular, the instructor illustrated belittling words, and emotional neglect, areas often deemed insignificant and generally glossed over and ignored by unsuspecting people. He suggested children especially who have been continuously abused or neglected emotionally might have subconsciously "stuffed" the hurt feelings to cope with injury to his or her inner spirit. He told us that if we were unable or did not know how to process those feelings in a healthy way when it happened, we might be subconsciously reacting to present hurtful incidents the unhealthy way we learned to live with the pain. That made a lot of sense, reading practically the same thing from "**The Source Of My Strength**" reinforcing the importance to continue the search of memories that injured my spirit. I struggled as I continued my pursuit, not knowing what was blocking my thoughts.

New Freedom

Our church invited Dr. Neil Anderson founder of "freedom In Christ" ministry to present us with a life-changing truth he discovered studying the scriptures, a two-day seminar. Once again, it was my weekend off and I eagerly attended.

We met in the sanctuary the first day of the seminar. We watched a short video clip of how **Freedom In Christ** Ministry came to be, and how God has used this ministry to help thousands of Christians learn to have a closer walk with God by; as my pastor so succinctly described, "cleaning our spiritual houses," sins we forgot or buried, sins still present and offensive to God. Dr. Anderson told us how he started out as a young man in aeronautics as an engineer and wound up teaching theology. He stumbled on a profound truth and developed the **steps to freedom**, a seminar to help Christians break the spiritual and mental strongholds in their lives. **Hidden sin**, pride, excuses, denial, deep seeded resentment and traumatic experiences are some of the roadblocks that prevent Christians from experiencing a deep abiding relationship with God; and because God is holy, can not look upon sin. Until we confess and process the hidden sin and renounce it from our lives, we fall short of the "heart of God" relationship that we desire to have with our Heavenly Father. Isaiah 43: 25, I John 1:9 assures we are forgiven of sin when we invite Christ to live in us. As long as we keep prayed up and confessed up we can and do approach the Throne of our Heavenly Father. Ah! but to experience a more **intimate relationship with Him** there is another step we must take, sadly, too often we settle for the former state of relationship. What effect does "hidden" sin in our lives have on our mental/spiritual state of mind? Dr. Anderson suggests those hidden sins are what Satan uses to keep us in spiritual bondage, stuck emotionally to that time in life and separated from the deeper depth of relationship to "the heart of God". He continued, most Christians reject his theory until they go through the steps to spiritual freedom.

Not remembering hurtful childhood experiences and having been divorced twice, I believed I could never attain the intimate "heart" relationship with God I so deeply yearned for. I heard myself saying, "I can't remember my past", and "God would never accept me", words that repeated in my thoughts when I tried to get in touch with past memories. I listened attentively, hanging on to every word Dr. Anderson shared. Most times in the past, I would get lost mentally trying to grasp concepts, but Dr. Anderson conveyed truth so simply, I understood what he was saying. Eventually I learned Satan cleverly manipulated my thoughts to discourage me in my pursuit to grow and learn the truth. It became clear that he used many attractive things to keep my mind occupied, far from spiritual answers to truth and healing. Ephesians 6:12, (my paraphrase) we wrestle not against each other in flesh and blood but against principalities and powers of the air... in the spirit realm. Dr. Anderson also told us that Satan:

First... disguises wounded emotions (past and present) so we deny and excuse because we are not consciously aware, and

Second... manipulates our thoughts to draw us away from our spiritual focus and godly responses; causing reactions toward a confrontation or offense, irrational negative thinking motivates retaliation and an unchristian like reaction toward an offender. It usually turns out to be the defensive verbal or physical attack we learned as children. Our reaction could also be silent, depending on the unhealthy learned behavior that got us through the confrontation at the time. **Mature Christians especially, fall prey to** the evil one's clever ways of subtle deception. Unconsciously unaware, Satan uses our intellect as a deterrent many times to keep our thoughts imprisoned with excuses and denial. Making excuses is a stronghold that blinds our spiritual eyes to acknowledge the raw truth we need to confess and renounce. Denial is a stronghold that prevents us from hearing, understanding and processing the truth; both in turn lead to continual sin not confessed. That is Satan's goal for the Christian, to set up and/or maintain a "spiritual stronghold", any way he can to keep us in a mental prison and separated from having a deep abiding relationship with God our Father. His success lies in his cleverness to fool the mature Christian into thinking such truth is foolishness. A Christian's maturity can be stuck in a time of life when a traumatic experience occurred. Satin does his best to keep the stronghold steadfast preventing the unknowing Christian from further growth until the traumatic experience is discovered and processed. Several spiritual strongholds were preventing me from *remembering* incidents that injured my spirit deeply planted in the early years of my life. That, in turn, kept me from *growing and maturing* in my spiritual life. Each time hurtful incidents occurred in my childhood it produced a "bitter fruit seed" to germinate in my little girl years. My emotions were stuck to the time in my life when those specific hurtful incidents took root because I was too young and unaware, unable to resolve any spiritual and emotional trauma at the time. In my adult years, I learned to cope with hurt feelings by substituting "wants", busyness," and "blaming others", a behavior I repeated many times throughout my life. In my twenties, I also believed I was flawed beyond acceptance by God and thought I could never attain the privilege of a close relationship with Him like the other people that attended church all the time. The evil one blackmailed my thought process and kept me in spiritual bondage for many years. Present hurtful incidents triggered "original unresolved issues". Divorce created deep emotional trauma, which triggered the emotional feeling of abandonment from my childhood, one of the many strongholds I would discover in my search for answers. The unprocessed feeling of abandonment in my childhood deeply scarred my emotions. I realized there must be many unresolved issues I was not aware of, remembering the negative words that described my behavior on the bitter fruit tree in class. I was also relieved to learn The Holy Spirit has access to and reveals the real truth worldly counseling can not disclose. God heals the total person mentally/emotionally/spiritually.

We must do our part and make every effort to seek spiritual guidance and help; God will provide healing as we persistently ask, seek and knock. Matthew 7:7. We must not sit and wait for healing to just happen.

We were gathered in the church auditorium that day and Dr. Anderson asked us to bow our head, close our eyes, pray a simple prayer and ask The Holy Spirit to show us what was spiritually blocking us from having a closer relationship with God. Dr. Anderson stated as The Holy Spirit brings situations to mind, Satan will be opposing the validity of importance. Satan attacks through intellect. He will try to get us to think, "Oh that's silly, you don't need to confess that," or "that happened when you were a child, every kid goes through that… simple child's play…that's not important enough to confess." Dr. Anderson stated we must acknowledge and process everything The Holy Spirit reveals, confess our offensive behavior; ask God to forgive our involvement, whether it was intentional or unknowing; renounce the sin or activity from our lives, then pray for the grace to forgive the offenses of others against us.

Pondering my past, a variety of pleasant memories flashed through my mind, the music we listened to in our home came first. My brothers tuned to popular and country, Sunday afternoons we listened to opera, Polish and Hungarian music my dad had playing on the radio when we came home from church. I loved it all, music made me feel happy. When I grew a little older, violin instrumentals captured my attention.

I prayed to remember unpleasant memories then waited...nothing came to mind. My thoughts drifted to several conversations I had with Florence, my sister in Christ, and good friend for many years. It always amazed me how she could remember many incidents in her childhood, I remembered little of mine. I thought I had a warm, loving, happy childhood and should have been able to remember more. Focusing back to the agenda at present, I became frustrated that I could not recall childhood experiences. Major portions of my teen years were also a blur.

Again, I prayed. A strangely familiar, yet daunting uneasiness came over me. "You don't remember because you are feeble-minded and forgetful," came from my thoughts. I sat back and closed my eyes for a few moments trying to get comfortable. Fearful feelings surfaced and questions bombarded my thoughts. If I was "daddy's girl" and spoiled rotten, why did I frequently feel so alone and abandoned? Why did I feel I would lose the people I loved and needed in my life? Why was I afraid to converse with people, try new things? Why did I feel inferior? Why did I feel childlike even to the people that were younger than I ? Why did I feel paralyzed when I needed to make decisions? Why was I too shy at school to eat lunch with the other kids in the cafeteria? Questions, feelings of frustration and abandonment whirled around and around in my mind adding confusion to my thought process, paralyzing efforts to reach the core. After a few more moments of prayer, the answer came. I remembered Dr. Anderson telling us to be aware of the thoughts we hear in our mind. That was the enemy's weapon to imprison our mind. As I continued to pray, The Holy Spirit illuminated a profound, spiritual stronghold Satan had on me. I began to feel that same familiar uneasiness I pushed aside so many times before, because I was not consciously aware of constant negative thoughts that controlled and added

38

to my already stressed emotions. Overly self-conscious about my inability to communicate my true feelings or opinions to anyone, I became highly stressed, my thoughts became confused, and childlike behavior would be the result of my actions. I was unable to grow and mature emotionally and spiritually because of the strongholds, Satan had control of for many, many years. "Confusion's" task was to lock my thought process so I couldn't resolve conflicts. I was relieved to learn it wasn't the lack of intelligence blocking my progress; it was the constant negative words playing repeatedly; the same crippling thoughts that controlled my behavior. Where did they come from?

The Pollution Comes Forth

Gradually, scrambled memories began to surface; portions of my childhood became clear and I recalled times I felt so desperately alone, needing someone to help process incidents that were upsetting as a young child. Little traumas were monumental to me. To many knowing parents, the early years from birth to age five are crucial years, where our unique personality and emotional stability takes place, where the development of trust and personal boundaries are established, but I don't think my mom or dad were aware. My parents were preoccupied dealing with their own problems economically, I just happened to be a part of their struggle to survive in this world. I believe people taking care of me did not realize my emotional need to express and process hurt feelings, fear, anxiousness, or answer the myriad of questions I asked. Those familiar "why?" and "how come?" questions that our children confronted us with, were not adequately explained when I was very young. I will venture to guess they thought I had too many "whys" and "how comes" and were dismissed with "oh, she'll get over it," consequently I was allowed to grow up instead of being nurtured.

An imaginary friend helped me cope with childhood fears. I do not remember exactly when I invited it into my thoughts. In the beginning, the imaginary friend was kind and loving, and it seemed to get me through hurtful incidents. A short time later, that friend turned and twisted little traumas inward attacking my intellect. Negative messages accused me of being dumb or wrong. "Shut up, don't say anything, you'll make a fool of yourself, you don't really know anything." Confusion joined and bound thought processes, thwarting my ability to reason sensibly, making it difficult to express myself. I believed I was inferior, different.

Sitting silently praying, tears began to flow. A humiliating degrading experience so deeply "stuffed" in my subconscious surfaced. The boy's name came to mind first, then his laughter; next, I relived the incident. I was walking on the side of the road past his house. Laughing, he called to me out of a tree. As I looked up, warm water hit my skin; he urinated on me! Why did he do it? Sobbing I looked to see if anyone saw what happened. I wept as I sat in the auditorium reliving that painful incident I completely blocked from memory. I prayed and asked God to heal my wounded spirit then found myself forgiving that boy and released the offense.

My mother spanked me when I disobeyed. I do not remember her being excessive; I do remember what she said before I was punished. I was told I was a bad girl for misbehaving, not that I was a good girl doing something bad; another prayer forgiving belittling words, releasing that hurt. I confessed to rebellious behavior then prayed for healing from inferiority.

My father had a unique way of treating my disobedience. He put his hand upon my shoulder and spoke my name in a low voice, wrinkled his forehead to a frown, shook his head from side to side and clicked his tongue, which I interpreted he was ashamed of me. The spankings from my mom and the repetitious reaction from my father I interpreted as shame, now deeply seated in my subconscious mind. I mentally replayed offensive behavior continually striving to figure a way to make up for disappointing them. I prayed again confessing disobedience to my parents, then asked my Heavenly Father to heal my damaged emotions and release me from the bondage of shame and a false sense of inadequacy.

Fearful of losing friends I felt I needed to please people so they would like me. Good deeds usually were unobserved. When others received credit, it invalidated my participation and I acted out rebelliously, then later thought about my behavior and felt sorry for acting badly.

In my teen years, I followed my peers examples, only to find out I could not reverse decisions to do more than I should have gotten involved with at a young age. Later, I woefully regretted my actions. Guilt added more stress to my emotions and played a vital role in the direction I chose to travel.

Three books I read that Dr. Anderson wrote helped shed light on insecurities from my past. Mental confusion became a permanent obstacle, growing stronger as stress increased. I strived to communicate and mentally fought through thought processes struggling for the right words to answer questions or state my point of view. Mentally paralyzed from lies that began in my childhood, my tightly wound emotions spun up and down like a yo-yo.

The bitter spiritual seeds that took root in my childhood had many years to grow stronger. I had deeply planted weeds of fear, lack of self-control, shame, jealousy, greed, envy, strife, and rejection. Stress was the catalyst that triggered confusion then defensive behavior. I projected blame to other people when my plans went awry. When my intelligence was threatened, I had to defend myself from feeling inferior at any cost, and the learned defensive behavior that I displayed in retaliation, was the way I reacted as an adult.

Stress caused a domino like effect on my emotions. When I had to make decisions, confused thoughts led to juggle opposing resolutions resulting in hasty decisions. Consequences from poor decisions imprinted emotional panic when I realized I made a wrong choice. Childhood fears emerged, bound my emotions and numbed my capability to think beyond my failure to make a right choice. By the time I reached my preteen years I convinced myself I couldn't make it through life on my own, and clung to people believing if I held on tight enough I could make it through on their talents and attributes. I lived my life hitchhiking on the shirttails of other people's accomplishments. My mind was continuously preoccupied emotionally, trying to defend myself and fix mistakes. **In prayer, I renounced that "special friend" and all of its' influence.**

Dr. Anderson suggested several items that children from our era played with and he held up a "magic eight ball". I did not think that innocently playing with a magic ball could be harmful. It was a high priority item to have back in the fifties. The ball was an object Satan used as another stronghold, to bind one to occult activity playing with it. I had completely forgotten I had one too. I asked my mom to buy it for me. I prayed. I confessed and renounced all evil influence from playing with it. You may be saying to yourself at this point, "Oh that's silly, I wouldn't go that far." With what I learned of Satan's tricks to keep your spirit in bondage, yes you do have to go that far to be free of his evil influence in your life. I learned how the evil one can disguise hidden sin in a Christian's life so cleverly that any one would not even think that insignificant toys we played with from our childhood could be a significant factor blocking us from access to a deeper relationship with God our Father.

I had forgotten other occult activity I was involved in as a teen. Renouncing the influence of the magic ball was the key that unlocked the following deeper memories that came after renouncing the ball. I remembered having been involved with a group of kids that dabbled in witchcraft, accomplishing incredible feats after performing a special ceremony. I confessed and renounced each activity and the evil influence and affect it had on my spirit.

A children's sermon, came to mind about a man who passed by a certain pet shop every day after work. He often glanced in the window to see what animal or creature they were featuring. One day while passing by he noticed the employee had a large snake draped on his shoulder, it caught his attention, continued on home; but he could not forget the image. The next day, he decided that if he saw the snake in the window again he would take a closer look. Wouldn't you know it? The clerk and snake were in the window. He went into the shop and asked questions, coming away learning snakes make fascinating pets. The man began to entertain the idea that having a snake would make him popular with his friends. He decided to purchase a small one. He brought it home, put it in a large container and took care, exercising, and feeding it live mice. He thought feeding live mice was gross at first but he grew used to the idea the mouse had to die for his pet to live. After a while, he became insensitive to the plight of the tiny mice and instead, enjoyed watching the snake eat them alive. Any pang of remorse he felt for the mice he excused by saying it was survival of the fittest. He spoke the truth. Each day the Boa exercised by wrapping itself around the man's arm. It gave a gentle squeeze then fell to the table. Months passed, the boa matured, so did it's wild instinct, unbeknown to the man. He had faith and trusted it would not harm him and allowed the snake to wrap itself around his body. True to creation, one day the snake instinctively squeezed the living breath from the man and he died. Pastor said sin is like that boa, ever present in the world around, enticing us. Satan knows he can't have our heart, so he sets traps, temptations, seemingly harmless at first, then stronger, (thinking, then wanting, then making excuses and rationalizing why we should), when we obtain what we think we want, it takes our focus away from God and onto ourselves and adds more wants to our wish lists. When we loose our focus of God we feel guilty resulting in spiritual separation. Satan succeeds because he caused a delay in the plan God has designed for our lives. **The story reminds us to be on guard each moment each day, because the enemy is always ready to steal the joy and peace that God gives us if we keep our focus on Him.**

The Holy Spirit illuminated areas that I needed to be aware of.

Mistaken Confidence

I thought back to my infant state of being born again. My whole world was new and thrilling. Spiritually, I celebrated my salvation, Christ forgave me for ALL my sin, I was free! I had no idea I subconsciously harbored emotional insecurities that lay hidden in my heart. Satan was well aware of that fact, and in a few short months after my conversion, the evil one began working on my thoughts and a subtle deception took place. Even though I read my bible and memorized scripture, I gave no quality time to let God speak to me through scripture and prayer, leaving me with head knowledge, and so very little heart knowledge, I was a baby Christian then and for many years after. Stressful times resurrected insecurity and inferiority. The two drove me to strive for perfection, as I grew older, sometimes to the extreme of being compulsive. I recalled many times as a child shouting "He made me do it, it's his fault." People that I loved and cared for who did not see my point of view I surmised were just not as spiritually mature. I was right, they were wrong; it was that simple. I found myself still using, "it wasn't my fault", to excuse poor choices, projecting blame to others. I was emotionally out of control with a distorted view of my spiritual self. Christ slipped from first place to second, what I failed to see was, instead of JESUS and me-- it was ME and Jesus. I substituted Jesus with my husband, children and things. God wanted me to love Him with **all** my heart, with **all** my soul, with **all** my body, and have no other gods before Him.

Sitting in the auditorium, it became obvious that the nagging voice from that "imaginary friend" never left me, not in my childhood, nor in my teen or young adult years, not even in my thirties, forties or early fifties, cleverly hidden in my subconscious memory. For the first time **I was able to identify negative thoughts that had a stranglehold on**

45

my mind. Going through **The Freedom** seminar allowed God's Spirit to illuminate incidents that injured my spirit, issues from the depths of my being. I began to clearly identify stress as the catalyst that brought out the "root" childhood fears which influenced my adult behavior. **Confusion imprisoned my thoughts** and I could not differentiate between the prompting of the Holy Spirit and the voice that controlled my mind. **I know now that fear and anxiety controlled my behavior.**

As I learned to identify and confront the strongholds that imprisoned my mind, The Holy Spirit and I began to tear down the wall in my heart through years of holding grudges, making poor choices blaming others, and making excuses. God's Word and the Holy Spirit empowered me to forgive others and myself and enabled me to replace lies with the truth, healing painful memories. I renounced sinful practices, horror movies I viewed, pictures of pornography, drinking, swearing, using Jesus' Name in vain, I also recalled a visit to a psychic in my early twenties. I renounced all evil from that visit; I confessed each sin, each memory. I gave it all to Jesus. Emotional exhaustion, baggage I carried from remorse and guilt, melted away and released their grip from my spirit.

It is important to **acknowledge any recalled incident and/or sin audibly**, no matter how foolish or trivial, and **renounce** each issue, to be free of its influence **and** future influence. Most importantly, I needed to **confess** those issues to God **to have a right relationship with Him, in order to grow, mature and have the freedom to worship, and to respond to people in a healthy way.** My Loving Heavenly Father patiently waited for this erring child to seek Him for guidance. In His wisdom, He knew what I needed and led me to this very point in my life.

One chapter in The Source of My Strength dealt with emotional guilt. Two painful memories kept replaying in my mind, my son running away from me after an altercation in the basement many years ago, for one. I especially wanted to make up for that. Another was when my grown daughter confided a deep secret she harbored for years. We were parked, abut to go shopping when she blurted out unbelievable occurences and sobbed uncontrollably through emotionally charged declaration everything that transpired. Emotionally driven, I needed to repay her for those terrible experiences. Feeling responsible, I tried to fix their wounded spirits monetarily, unable to forgive myself for allowing those horrible experiences to occur, the very things I fretted would happen.

False guilt motivated me to protect them from experiencing consequences they should have gone through as they encountered life struggles, doing more harm to them and myself. I became their enabler. Apprehensive not knowing what the future held for each of my children, I knew I needed to let go. In faith, I placed them in God's hands knowing God has been and still is in control of their lives. My job is to pray for them. I cling to His promise that if we train up a child in the way he should go, when they are old he will not depart from it. Proverbs 3: 5 and 6.

As a geriatric nurse, I see many elderly people who did not or could not resolve their childhood traumas at an earlier stage of their lives. Most go through the dying process tormented by fear of painful memories that are "locked in their mind" from dementia or Alzheimer's disease. You must face those painful areas to free your spirit while you still have the capability. Seek God with all your heart. He wants to heal and "grow you up." Acknowledge your sins, I John 1:9 says If we confess our sins He is faithful and just to forgive our sins and cleanse us from all unrighteousness. God will not condemn you, ask forgiveness with a repentant heart, learn from your mistakes and go on...Jesus promised He would never leave you. God created us with three unique needs; physical, emotional and spiritual. He blesses us with work to fulfill the physical,, the emotional and spiritual only God can fill. When you invite the Holy Spirit into your life, He fills the spiritual need for love and acceptance. The more earnestly you trust God the more complete you will experience love and acceptance in your spirit resulting in a deep abiding peace and joy in your heart. No one or nothing else can fill that void. The first of the Ten Commandment in the bible says to have no other gods before Him.

Returning to our adult bible class, we then studied "Boundaries", by Dr. Henry Cloud and Dr. John Townsend. My mind soaked up valuable information I missed learning to set my own and respect others' boundaries in my childhood and young adult years. I unknowingly invaded the personal boundaries of my family and allowed others to step over mine. I was not aware that I had freedom to **respond** to others instead of **reacting** to others. I did not know what responding and reacting meant. Learning I had a right to my own opinion and others had a right to theirs, I could say no and be happy about it, and I had to accept a no answer from others. I am so thankful for the wonderful ladies in our class whom we experimented and practiced our personal boundary lines before we applied them to outsiders. Boundaries has given me freedom to express myself and respect others freedom to do the same. Hindsight is painful but it gives twenty-twenty vision to recognize unhealthy behaviors I passed to my children. When opportunities arise to share what I learned, I am thankful I can help them.

Spiritual Personality Strengths

Another vital step toward healing was discovering how my personality, flawed as I saw it could be an asset to furthering God's Plan. God knew that too, and led me to another steppingstone.

During Adult Bible Fellowship hour, our Assistant Pastor handed out a questionnaire to anyone who wished to know what his or her spiritual gifts were. I was curious to know what mine were, and took the test. God again made available a way to get His message across to me that He gave me the very gifts and personality He chose, to be equipped for the work He planned for me to do for Him; to nurture others God puts in my path to interact and point them to faith in Christ and salvation. Knowing my spiritual gifts is not something I made up but true gifts from my Heavenly Father encouraging me to press on to the higher calling He designed for such a time as this. I took another test, which revealed my spiritual strengths.

The seminars, classes and experiences God led me through changed my life; steppingstones that brought me to the present. God's Word continues to be alive and true...Romans chapter 8, verse 28 reads, "And we know that all things work together for good to those who love God to those who are the called according to His purpose."

Why Me? God's Answer

Proverbs, 1-8 My son if you accept my words and store up my commands within you, turning your ear to wisdom and applying your heart to understanding, and if you call out for insight and cry aloud for understanding, and if you look for it as for silver and search for it as for hidden treasure;, then you will understand the fear of the LORD and find the knowledge of God. For the LORD gives wisdom and from **His mouth** come knowledge and understanding. He holds victory in store for the upright, He is a shield to those whose walk is blameless, for He guards the course of the just and protects the way of His faithful ones.

The windows of memory, false beliefs about "the innocent years of childhood", and seeing the method the evil one used to disguise portions of my recall caused me to become more keenly aware of the world's strong and subtle influence to divide, conquer and take my spiritual focus away from God.

When I gave up seeking human solutions and directed full concentration to God for help and was willing to face and admit difficult truth issues I really did not want to believe about myself, then and only then was my question answered. I received the answer to the "why" question I kept asking God. Listening to the crippling voice from my youth feeding lies to my thoughts, I could plainly see where I made erroneous assumptions throughout my marriage. I did not heal from childhood fears, anxieties and disappointments and they strongly influenced my behavior and the choices I made. I did not plan a relationship filled with turmoil. Stress was the catalyst that resurrected emotional abandonment and insecurity, and motivated reactions to many marital conflicts. Not being able to communicate true feelings caused many misunderstandings. It was extremely difficult to face the truth and admit that I contributed to the breakdown of our marriage but I was not going to let the evil one steal my joy and peace as I processed painful memories and accepted responsibility where I needed to confess my error. Going through the painful process of searching for answers was necessary, God had to be my only focus, the only One I could depend on, the One I would find the depth of peace and joy in, and never have to search for another love to fill the vacancy that used to be in my heart. Scripture assured me that I was not inferior. I read in the first chapter of Ephesians how much God valued me. Psalm 139 is an assurance of God's unconditional love. Jesus never once abandoned me.

Although my initial motivation was to prove my innocence to the breakdown of our marriage, God lovingly changed my heart and the path I chose to follow. He refined me into a whole person, with a new direction. God blessed me with a unique life story to share with others. I could not change one detail; it continues to be part of a much bigger plan. Discovering the truth from various programs but ultimately from God's Word freed me from the bondage of my past. Forgiving those who hurt me has released my spirit to love others unconditionally just as Jesus forgives and loves us unconditionally. I have a deep abiding love for my Heavenly Father and an inner depth of peace in my soul no one or nothing can take away. I know nothing can separate me from God my Father, my life is His to do with what He chooses. I trust and believe He has molded and changed me into a new person; not who I used to be, serving myself, but one that has found true happiness, joy and peace serving the King of Kings and Lord of Lords. I am still growing in Him daily. My journey has just begun and each day is a new day, with new beginnings.

Christ is the ultimate answer to meet our needs and heal our broken hearts. He is our bridge to God and the source of the deep abiding peace we all can experience in our very souls. He gives us joy in the midst of trial while we live and mingle with others here on earth. We are here to be stepping-stones to help others on their journey through this life to lead people to salvation in Christ.

Jeremiah 29:11 God said, "For I know the plans I have **for you,** declares the Lord, plans for your welfare and not for calamity to give you a future and a hope". He gathered the pieces of my broken life and lovingly put them together to make the unique person that I am today, to pass hope on to you.

Encouraged, and compelled, I was eager to go back to the beginning, the very beginning to fill in the gaps of forgotten memories from my past.

Journaling: A Way to Remember

I decided to journal everything I could recall. Journaling also jogged forgotten memories. The Holy Spirit helped me work through painful incidents and pointed to many areas where I made excuses blaming others when things didn't work out the way I wanted because of poor choices I made. Blinded by the distorted image of myself, I couldn't handle being wrong about anything; I twisted truth and tried to manipulate situations until I thought they would work out the way I planned.

Family history was the most important piece of the puzzle I was about to put together. It was important for me to know what each of my parents childhood was like, how they were treated; generational beliefs, traditions, habits, anything that would shed light on my parents and grandparents behavior. I wanted to have a clearer understanding of my family roots, to break any negative chain of neglect and if possible to put an end to passing on generational dysfunctions.

Unfortunately, I didn't ask my parents questions about our family history, what life was like for them growing up long ago. I did not think to ask my mother questions about our family history when I got older. I was not inquisitive to ask her about my birth... the stories women share with each other about giving birth and labor pains, when I had my children. The only story I heard, true or not, was that my father desired to have a little girl, and he named me after a radio program that was popular back in the forties. I thought my mom would be around for many years and I had plenty of time to ask all those questions later. I was presumptuously wrong. When I needed her most in my life she died of cancer. She was only fifty-seven. I was twenty-seven years old. I deeply mourned her leaving me at a time when I needed her most in my life. I prayed again, this time for healing and forgiveness on my part for offensive behavior toward my mom. Even though she had passed away several years before I prayed that prayer, it was healing to ask forgiveness. In my spirit I felt somehow my mother would know.

My mom and dad passed away before I became aware that within them, was a wealth of their family history. The memories and stories I learned is second hand and only a small portion of the past I can pass on in a written record. Realizing that fact, I became more encouraged to write.

My prayer is for my children and grandchildren to see the process of God's faithfulness in drawing me spiritually into the plan He has for my life, and to grasp the trust I have in God to guide my family and future generations to find, trust and follow His plan for their lives. Although I made wrong choices and had to pay the consequence for my error, He never left me. Where I strayed, I can see where He gently guided my footsteps back into His plan. Every experience shaped me into the person He created me to be. Laugh and cry with me through the joys and struggles I had in the beginning of my life, and experience with me where I believe, I started to become aware of God as He revealed Himself to me. Through this manuscript, it is my desire to convey to my grandchildren especially, the absolute necessity of having a "personal faith" in God, then to my children and others who are inspired to read on; how vitally important it is to trust Him and respond to His gentle nudges traveling through life. God is patient, loving, merciful and most of all, forgiving. In simple to read language, it is my hope to reveal God's faithfulness. Although I felt abandoned by others, He never once abandoned me through the years. He gave me a free will, a choice to follow Him or go my own way. He has always protected me to this present day and continues to mold my character into His Divine Will.

Accepting Christ into my heart powerfully changed my life and set me on a narrow road that few travel. In the Bible in Proverbs 21:19 it says, "The mind of man plans his way, but the Lord directs his path." In Psalm 139, from the New Living Bible verses 13 - 16. You made all the delicate, inner parts of my body and knit me together in my mother's womb. Thank you for making me so wonderfully complex! Your workmanship is marvelous—and how well I know it. You watched me as I was being formed in utter seclusion, as I was woven together in the dark of the womb. You saw me before I was born. Every day of my life was recorded in your book. Every moment was laid out before a single day had (yet) passed.

I turned on my computer and as it booted up I sat, hands on the keyboard praying to God to help me work through painful memories as they came to mind, to continue healing my heart, and spirit. I wondered what I would discover in my endeavor to revisit my childhood.

My Childhood Environment

I was born just before World War II ended in January 1944, third and last child in birth order to my siblings, both older brothers. Joey was eight years older and Gigi, ten years older than I was. They became my primary caregivers during the week because my mother had to work to support us.

My mom, dad, two brothers, our dog, and I lived in a five-room apartment in a government owned housing complex in Connecticut, I thought the perfect place for any kid to live. There were plenty of woods to explore but not enough to get lost, swamps where I caught tad poles in the spring, hayfields to run around in, vacant lots we used to ride our bikes in, and steep hills for all kinds of play. I had no boundaries, the entire neighborhood was mine to explore. The only requirement to have a good time was imagination. There was always something to get involved in.

Three major roads ran through the project. The main road leading to the houses split three ways at the entrance. One, continuing upward through the middle, one going right to the backside, and one going left to the front. Off to the left of the main road, towards the back of the complex was a little park in a vacant lot, where a group of teenage volunteers taught us handcrafts and played baseball in the summer. We called it "summer school." The park department installed a large metal swing set that I loved to swing on for hours. A dirt path, wide enough for one car, leading out of the complex and into another government housing project ran between two swampy areas to the back of the vacant lot. In the winter a group of us who didn't know how to skate well, slid around holding on to the trees, trying to skate over the hay stubble mounds that protruded through the murky ice.

The road turned right at the park forming a loop, then joined the back road leading out of the complex. Often people walking or driving would cut through our development saving about a mile or so of travel time. One of my mother's sisters lived "up the hill" as I described giving directions to people who asked where a certain address was. Another of her sisters lived "over the hill" because in my back yard one had to go up and over a gently rolling hill to get to the middle road where my aunt lived. Geographically, I lived somewhere in the middle and in the front. Sounds confusing but everyone that lived there understood those directions.

A large sloping vacant lot up the hill from my back yard was one of my favorite places to play after school and in the summer. Baseball games and tag were a favorite past time. In the winter, snowstorms were plentiful and deep soft snow blanketed the hill and streets. We had fun from early morning to late at night sledding because not only did we sled down that hill, but also all the way down to the end of the road that led to the project complex. It took three to five minutes for the sled ride to the end. The tiring side of that was it took twice as long to walk back, but it was worth it. I had the best environment any kid could want.

Back in the "olden days" when I was a kid, a milkman drove to our house in a white truck and delivered glass quart bottles of fresh whole milk. In the wee early hours of the morning, I'd hear the clanging of bottles against the metal case the milkman used to carry several at once. At night, customers would leave their empties on their porch with a slip of paper specifying the quantity they would need next delivery. Before he drove off he would holler, "milkman." Milk was much fresher and creamier than what we buy in the store today. I watched my mom open a new bottle at breakfast; after she removed the smooth white cardboard cap the thick white cream that settled at the top of the bottle, she poured into a small drinking glass, and she and my dad used it for their coffee in the morning.

Another man delivered kerosene for our kitchen stove. My mom and brothers were the only ones that could fill the kerosene container that fit snugly into its special holder along side the kitchen stove. In order to work properly, it had to sit on the holder just right. When I asked if I could help my mom told me, I was too young and clumsy. The kerosene was kept outside in a drum that was propped up off the ground by a large steel cradle it sat on out behind the coal bin. I often played cowboys and Indians sitting on top of it. I smuggled the small rug my mom hung out to air on the clothesline, threw it over the huge barrel and used it like a saddle, pretending the barrel was my horse. Many times, I used the spout to mount the barrel often spilling a good portion of kerosene, repeatedly reminded to keep off the drum. When I did not listen, I received a spanking.

We burned coal in the furnace to heat our home and my mom ordered it by the half-ton. It was stored in a large bin on our back porch. Just a tot at the time, I discovered the coal bin one day while playing on the porch. Curiosity prompted me to explore and I peeked in to investigate what was in that dark mysterious place, then climbed in to get a first hand feel of the soft black pieces of coal. My mom called and before I could scramble out, she found me, blackened head to foot from the dust particles; another spanking. When I was a little older than too young, my job was to scoop out the ashes from the little door at the bottom of the furnace after the fire died down.

On warm rainy summer days, I ran, splashing through the streams of water that trickled down the side of the street. After a soaking rain, I'd plunk myself down alongside the black rubber tire "planter" my mom had half buried in our front yard and scooped up handfuls of mud forming it into neat little pies. She often caught me eating the mud pies. I'd smile sheepishly as she chastised me. On chilly rainy days, I sat at the kitchen table with my brothers after they came home from school and listened to the radio. Their favorite programs were mysteries and comedies, "The Shadow" and "Amos and Andy" to name a few. My mom liked "Molly Goldberg," and "Stella Dallas". My dad liked opera music, but often made fun of female vocalists when he thought she held a note too long. I giggled when he made funny comments in Hungarian not knowing what he said.

Television came into being when I was four years old. In 1953, my mom bought our very first TV. I was mesmerized as I watched puppet shows like "Kukla, Fran and Ollie", "Cecil the Seasick Sea Serpent and his friend Beanie", and my favorite, "The Howdy Doody Show." I became one with the characters and episodes. One of the characters wore a black cape and hid his face behind it. He played bad tricks on nice people. The audience (dubbed the peanut gallery) were the first to warn the unsuspecting person by shouting. Clara Bell ran in pursuit of the villain honking her horn at him. I did not like him; he frightened me. Anxiety and fear from the emotionally charged scene, held my emotions captive. Even though everything turned out fine for the character on TV, repeated thoughts warned that the bad villain was going to get me next. My brothers and I watched the scary Alfred Hitchcock dramas on TV too, and fear continued to occupy and consume my thoughts. Bedtime was right after the TV programs ended. I acted silly shouting dumb things to my brothers as I started up the stairs, trying to cover up being afraid of the dark. They made weird sounds like squeaking doors and crows cawing. One hid at the top of the stairs, and as I neared the top step, he jumped out of the dark and frightened me. Typical of boys their age, they enjoyed scarring me and laughed as I reacted. I could feel the presence of fear as I ran down the hallway and jumped into bed. I pulled the blanket over my head to avoid being swallowed up by fear's presence. My brothers knew nothing about parenting or meeting the emotional needs of an overly sensitive little girl. I needed reassurance that I was safe, that there was nothing to fear. Instead, anxiousness confused my thoughts, I did not like being made fun of or frightened. They had no idea that fear and anxiety was what I wrestled with in my heart listening to harassing thoughts. I had a double portion of harassment, from crippling thoughts, to two brothers who seemed to enjoy scaring me half to death.

"Ordinary childhood play" you say. Yes, it was, but continuous pranks instilled feelings of insecurity, anxiety and fear, and stayed with me for a very long time. One would think I would "catch on" to their practical jokes, but I did not. I started building a protective emotional wall in my mind and it grew steadily and strong.

Negative thoughts from the imaginary friend I invited into my life earlier had a unique way of confusing my mind lulling me into a hypnotic state. Mental anxiety prevented me from processing any thought and I bit my fingernails until they bled.

In our home the living room and kitchen were on the first floor and all three bedrooms and the bathroom were on the second. The stairwell leading upstairs was narrow and dark. The bathroom was the first tiny room at the top of the stairs. Next to the bathroom was my parents' room, then, turning a sharp left going through a hallway next to their room was my brothers' room, then mine.

My tiny bedroom was a few feet bigger than the bathroom, and had a small window that overlooked our front yard and the street. A large alcove closet held my clothes, and was deep enough to play and hide from my mom when I broke her rules.

My brothers' bedroom was spacious and bright and I liked to play in their room. Their twin beds had metal headboards with vertical bars about six inches apart, and metal springs under the mattresses. I especially liked to jump up and down bouncing from one bed to the other. While playing one day, I wedged my head in between the bars of one of the headboards. The bars held my head tight; my ears grew hotter as I tried desperately to free myself while screaming for my brother. "Stupid, stupid" replayed in my thoughts as I struggled. My brother Joey came to my rescue and laughed when he saw the predicament I was in. I did not see any humor in the situation at the time. I pleaded with him to get me out. He observed a comical situation; he did not see how stupid I felt.

In the fifties and sixties, major childhood diseases consisted mainly of whooping cough, mumps, chicken pox, regular measles and German measles. Medicine for Polio was still in the experimental stage. I had two bouts of German measles, regular measles, whooping cough, chicken pox and mumps. At six years old, recovering from mumps, I woke up in the middle of the night with pain in my neck and could not move my head. My skin felt wet. As I searched for the source of pain, my hand gravitated toward a lump on the left side of my neck as big as an egg. I tried again to move my head but could not. I called for my mom. After feeling my forehead, she took my temperature, then hurried down the stairs and made several phone calls trying to reach a doctor. She contacted one that would see me in the middle of the night, bundled me up and drove me to his office. I still remember his name today. Dr. Bileau. He said silly things and popped his lower false teeth out to amuse me while he examined my neck. He told my mom I had an infected mastoid gland and needed immediate surgery. The doctor gave me a shot of Penicillin in each cheek of my buttocks and said he would meet us at the hospital. I remember lying across the top of the front seat of our car as she drove because I could not sit, my buttocks hurt from the big needles.

Two nurses greeted us at the emergency entrance. They transferred me onto a stretcher. I was happy to hear I could sit up during the tests. Then someone else wheeled me into another room and told me to lie down. Afraid and determined to stay seated, I stated the other nurse said I could sit up. When she tried to gently lay me down, I refused to cooperate. The nurse called for reinforcements. Everything happened so quickly when I saw other nurses enter the room, but sick or not I was ready for combat, and sat my ground. I was not happy anymore and fought with every ounce of strength I had in me to stay seated on that stretcher as I kicked and swung at them. I was a tough little girl and managed to make quite an impression on the doctor and nurses. My mom told me later it took four nurses to hold me while they tried to anesthetize me. To this day, I can still visualize that soft black rubber mask descending onto my face while I fought with every ounce of strength I had until I fell into a deep sleep.

God was there in the operating room protecting my life, guiding the doctor's hands, but I wasn't even aware of my Heavenly Father's presence back then. It took several months for my neck to heal. I enjoyed the weekly visits to that very special doctor and had fun playing a game with him each time he called me into his office. First, I sat down on the examination table and put my lower lip inside my top two front teeth then stuck out my upper lip and said, "What's up doc, you got false teeth?" He in return popped his false teeth out and made me laugh. God blessed that doctor in many ways, he was so patient and kind and knew just what to do to ease my fear.

Memories of My Dad

When I was a very young child, my dad had a special way to greet me upon entering the front door when he came home from work. "Where's my Roshmary?" The next question followed immediately after the first, "Whose girl are you?" Reaching out to hug him, greasy clothes and all I answered "daddy's girl". I felt special even if it was for a few brief moments. After his greeting, he headed straight for the kitchen stove, took a spoon out of the silverware drawer and ate cold food, scraping the pot to get the last morsel. Weekends when my mom was home; hearing him, she spoke a few words in Hungarian, I guessed she told him to stop scraping. My parents spoke Hungarian fluently and often said hurtful things to each other, which usually ignited a barrage of words, first in Hungarian then in English. When he grew tired of arguing he made a gesture as if to backhand my mom and told her to shut up. Without washing his face and hands or changing his clothes, he turned on the TV, sat in his squeaky rocking chair and smoked a couple of cigarettes, then kicked his shoes off just before he fell asleep. His feet smelled so terrible the odor cleared us from the room until the smell dissipated.

Hearing my parents say unkind things to each other often distressed me. I wished my mom and dad could be happy like my friends' parents, and not fight so much. I could not understand why or what they argued about, because they argued in Hungarian. When I grew older, I discovered they fought mostly over money.

My dad had the best of everything for his repair business. I knew that because I heard his friends say what great tools he had. He was a good mechanic and very generous to his customers. I remember looking through our family picture album; on one of the pages was an article cut from the newspaper about my dad being a Good Samaritan helping people who were stuck in the snow in the winter. It said he was so kind he accepted whatever people could afford and if they did not have money it was ok. I wondered why he was generous to strangers but did not contribute to the expenditures of running our home.

My father was not like any of my friends' dads. Like other kids, I depended on him when I needed advice; he answered with riddles and funny stories I thought totally unrelated to my questions. His answers did not make sense. Rephrasing my questions, I received the same response. I thought I was stupid because I could not figure out his answers. Frustrated, confused and disappointed I eventually stopped asking his advise.

I rode my bike five miles to my dad's garage when I was old enough to find my way back home. It was located off the main road in a wooded lot; a long dirt driveway led to his garage and a small creek ran through the back of the property. I watched him work on cars and listened to conversations he had with the men that hung around. My dad repaired the town's police cars free of charge. I thought because he never asked for payment they looked the other way when he broke the law driving, but in truth he had no regard for the law. One of the men that hung around his garage asked about the stop sign hanging on the wall, and he proudly replied he was stopped and ticketed for going through a stop sign. The night he paid the fine, he pulled the stop sign out of the ground and hung it up like a trophy in his garage. It was his, he stated, he paid for it. Overhearing some of his entanglements with the police, I boasted of his stories to my friends. My dad was "cool" because he had the nerve to tell cops off and take stop signs. I thought Hey! Look at me...I'm his daughter and I am "cool" too. He did not emulate good values and I clung to his "shirt-tails" to validate bad behavior in my rebellious teenage years.

Recalling another unforgettable incident, I believe negatively changed the direction in my life significantly. The first time I visited my father I checked out the garage. Two wooden double doors hung at either side of the large entrance. The dimly lit bay occupied a car my dad had been fixing, there was only a narrow pathway around it. The hood of the car was up with a light hanging under it obscuring my view to the back of the garage. As I looked down, I noticed the thickly stained floor smelled like motor oil. Curiosity drove me inside to explore further. I felt awkward as I gingerly edged my way along being careful not to step on the tools strewn on the floor. When I reached the back, I stopped, looked up and took a deep breath. Hanging on the wall were several calendars of bare women. I looked around, there were more, even hanging over my father's desk where he did his paperwork! I heard laughing and mumbling from the men outside as I gawked at the calendars. A burned impression of the bare women lingered in my thoughts for many years.

One of my father's friends owned a small gas station a few buildings down the road, across a vacant lot. He was not like my dad. His garage was bright, clean and the floors swept. His tools were clean and organized. I gazed around his garage, no nude pictures were hanging on his walls. A picture of a pretty calendar girl dressed in a red halter-top and shorts hung above his desk. He also displayed a picture of his wife and children on his desk. I recognized his son in the picture; we attended the same school. I liked to visit my father's friend because he was nice to me. He never failed to ask how I was doing in school. Seeing the difference between that man and my dad made me question why my father chose to display nude pictures on the walls of his garage where everyone could see them and preferred to work in a dirty environment. I wondered, but I never had the nerve to ask him.

Working through troubled memories, I wondered if those nude images were the catalyst that initiated a premature awareness of my body.

Enter Inferiority

I stood in the mirror one day, mentally comparing my body to the women on those calendars, remembering every detail of their flawless bodies. I had a weird shape; I was different. Every waking moment I thought about my flaw. I became extremely self-conscious and obsessively tried to hide the imperfection. While playing inside one day, I found a discarded brazier in a pile of old clothes and tried it on. I am embarrassed to say I stuffed the difference with cotton socks. I put a sweater on and stood admiring my figure in the mirror. Preoccupied, I was not aware of the comments made about my foolish behavior as I wore it everywhere. A very short time later, the undergarment disappeared. When I grew a little older, I again mentally compared myself to what I remembered of the pictures on those calendars. Disappointed, I was not developing as the girls I knew were, I hated my misshapen body, and blamed my dad because I inherited the same imperfection that he had been born with. A poor self-image plagued me for many years. I was so overly self-absorbed with the imperfection I had surgery years later to correct it.

Working Through Painful Memories

My father was sixty-three when he died of Congestive Heart Failure and passed away before I resolved the bitterness I harbored. As God began to heal my heart, I needed to forgive my dad even though he died years ago. I had to break the negative bonds that bound my spirit. In my pursuit to resolve ill feelings, I asked my aunt Irene, one of his sisters, what she remembered about my dad from her childhood. My paternal grandparents passed away before my birth, so I was curious to learn what they were like also. Irene, born in 1929, third to the last child, my dad already 29 and married to my mom, she could only relate family gossip, stories she heard from her older siblings.

Aunt Irene related most of what she remembered about my father; birth and death dates of her brothers and sisters and my grandparents. My dad was born in Hungary, February 1910. His mother was Protestant and his dad, Catholic. They came from a large family of eight sisters, two brothers and a set of twins totaling 13 children. They moved from Hungary to America when he was a young boy. His father was strict; when he spoke, they obeyed. A popular saying I recalled hearing from that generation, " children were seen and not heard", I thought, how awful it must have been for kids back then. My paternal grandmother had breast cancer and was bedridden when my aunt was a little girl. I cannot imagine the hardships they went through to survive day-to-day, the lack of quality medical care, plus living in a big family struggling through the Great Depression of 1929. Most children quit school to work before sixth grade to help their parents. In his youth, my dad wanted to become a musician, to play the violin, but his father opposed his dreams, the pay would not be enough to support him and put food on the table too. His hearts desire dashed, he bitterly resolved to work at something he really did not like. My dad had a chicken he

64

was fond of. His dad had to eventually butcher his pet to provide food for their large family. My father inherited his father's unwavering will and never ate chicken again until six months before he died, then asked for chicken at almost every meal. Unresolved hurts probably accumulated in his heart and he became bitter, I hardly ever saw him smile. He did not talk much unless he had something to say. He stood rigidly, the only time I saw him relax was when he came home and sat in his rocking chair.

I discovered that his method of escaping emotional pain was by telling riddles and funny stories and really could not relate to the opposite sex, to either my mom or me. His parents, siblings, and life situations strongly influenced him from the beginning of his childhood just as mine did. He had insecurities too, but he did not have the opportunity to resolve the pain and disappointment from his past. Parents pass negative as well as positive traits and insecurities to the next generation.

As the Holy Spirit enlightened my past, I recalled a pleasant memory from preteen years. My aunt Mary and uncle John were at our home celebrating one of the holidays. After we finished dinner, my uncle sat down at the piano and played a rather lively Hungarian song. My dad left the room and when he returned he was playing a violin. I never heard my dad play. It sounded wonderful. As memories flashed back, I recalled how relaxed and happy he was, he smiled and I thought I even remembered a twinkle in his eyes. I believe I saw my real father emerge from that hard outer shell he built around himself. The festivities imparted a lighthearted feeling; we were a happy family, if just for a brief few hours. My uncle and dad played for quite a while. I sat near the piano and watched my uncle's hands; his fingers looked like he was tickling the piano keys as they moved swiftly from one note to another. My dad, violin tucked under his chin, swayed from side to side with each stroke of his bow sliding across the slender strings. The music coming from the melancholy sounding notes of the last song they played sounded as though the notes coming from my dad's violin were crying. I closed my eyes and sadness came over me.

Learning of his hardships from my aunt gave me insight to forgive, to let go of bitterness and replace it with a pleasant memory. When I hear violin music, I think of my dad and smile knowing violin was his first love.

Insight

The odor of gasoline and oil still trigger those visual images and the painful old memories from my childhood. As a geriatric nurse, I observe elderly people reacting to unresolved issues in their lives. One word, one touch or action could set them off to mentally relive painful incidents as though they were going through their traumatic experience for the first time at any given moment. It's sad to see with most elderly people, senile dementia or Alzheimer's disease prevents their capability to process and resolve hurtful incidents and many go through the process of death agonized by their unresolved painful past. I concluded, if I had not worked through painful incidents they could continue to influence my behavior in the present, and on to old age. I thank God that He opened my spiritual eyes and heart to see the truth about others and myself.

Memories of Mom:
Love and Fun, With a Touch of Fear

My mom was born March 23, 1914. She was fourth in birth order to four brothers and five sisters. Mentally visualizing her thick dark eyebrows proportionately affixed over her sparkly, dark brown eyes, and her wiry, straight and salt and pepper colored hair, she was beautiful to me. Both of my parents had beautiful flawless skin; she enhanced her complexion by wearing bright red lipstick. I often watched as she applied it to her lips, then dabbed a small portion and smoothed it over her cheekbones to give them a blush. She stood about five foot four inches tall. Long dangling earrings graced her ears. I inherited her pleasingly plump figure. Her family experienced the depression of 1929 too, and they had very little when she was young; like my dad, she quit school to work contributing a portion of her pay to family needs. I did not think to ask about family history, her childhood, or what her interests were when she was alive. One of her sisters confided my mom worked as a housekeeper in her teen years.

Weekends were my mom's days off from working the evening shift three to eleven o'clock. I missed her during the week, the time we spent together Saturday and Sunday were special. Although I stated earlier, she often inappropriately threatened to do me bodily harm disciplining me, she was relentless in her efforts to instill good values in her children and she tried her best to keep me from doing anything I would be ashamed of later in my life. Raised in a Christian home, my mom had a reverential fear of God I did not see in my dad. Church was an important part of her life. Every Sunday she prepared dinner before we went to church. We stopped and bought Hungarian pastry at the bakery on our way home. The aroma from the dinner cooking as we walked in the door permeated the house and smelled so appetizing I could not wait to eat.

After dinner, dishes washed, dried and put away we visited her family. Occasionally my mom called her oldest sister on a weekday when she and my dad were not getting along. Sunday we visited the sister she called. My cousin and I played outside while my aunt and mom chatted. Retrieving a glass of water, I heard her crying. I wondered why my mom cried so often. Years later I learned she had been raped, gotten pregnant and had a baby at nineteen years of age. Having a baby in those days was a shame filled experience. My dad married her in exchange for a purse my grandfather offered. Having a baby so young changed the course of my mother's life, and strongly influenced the way she disciplined both of my brothers and me. I also concluded my brothers must have gone through great emotional turmoil living with a father who not only ignored them, but also did not show affection to my mom. Neither was equipped to meet our emotional needs, but in their own way, they tried. I believe my mom put more effort into raising us, especially faithful to make sure we attended church. I did discover she invited Jesus to live in her heart when she was a teen. She knew her inner strength came from having a personal faith in Jesus Christ as her Savior, and wanted us to learn that also.

My mom was spontaneous and fun loving and often surprised me with the way she reacted to my mischievous behavior, making lasting imprints on my emotions. I was an extremely difficult child, often taking confrontations to extreme, and came away from an incident with battered emotions most always drawing a wrong conclusion, emotionally influenced by degrading thoughts. I cannot remember if consistency was her norm, as she tried to enforce her rules with me but I knew I was in deep trouble when she called me "Sara Jane." That was not my name. Although she was not excessive, I feared punishment because she believed in not sparing the rod.

We cleaned house on Saturday. My job was to tidy my room and dust the living room furniture. We started early in the morning, by eleven o'clock all the housework was finished. She showered, changed her clothes and then we rode the bus to Bridgeport to pay weekly bills, occasionally accompanied by one of her sisters. The excursion downtown was exciting; we usually sat toward the back of the vehicle. My mom bought me a little trinket to compensate for guilt feelings I managed to inflict her conscience with when she left for work during the week. At noon, we stopped in one of the five and dime stores as they were nicknamed back then, and ate lunch. One afternoon after we finished eating, she sent me to the notions counter to buy sewing thread for her. Surprised, I hurried to the counter, picked the color she wanted then waited for the salesperson to take my money. The woman behind the counter continually ignored me when I tried to pay. After several attempts, I took the thread and gave it and the money to my mother. She brought me back to the counter and explained what she thought happened. My mom was not going to let me get away with stealing. Negative tapes played in my thoughts "thief, thief, that's what your mom thinks of you". I felt very bad. The woman blushed as my mom handed her the cash, never saying a word about ignoring me.

On our bus trip home I played with my "trinket" but wondered why she didn't pay attention when I tried to explain that I didn't steal the thread. Negative thoughts echoed my explanation didn't matter.

As I grew older, I became an expert at putting my mom on a guilt trip and demanded expensive toys. I asked for things that were more than she could afford. " I cried for an "English" bike, the latest fad. They had skinny tires, the brakes were on the handlebars and controlled the braking mechanism to the front tires instead of the back. My mom bought it, and I rode it a few times. Skidding in the sand was the latest fad. I tried skidding on my English bike and almost flipped forward over the handlebar. My mom asked why I stopped riding it. I told her I could not skid in the sand and didn't want the other kids to make fun of me. She uttered words that hurt me for forty-four years, "I wish I had ten boys instead of you." Looking back at my self-centeredness, I understood why she made that comment. Probably in utter exasperation, those words slipped out of her mouth as she tried to deal with my demanding selfishness, I was unfortunate enough to hear them. I lived as though the world revolved around me, me, me; unconcerned with hardships I put my mother through, as she gave in to my selfish greediness.

Saturday evenings, I cuddled in my mom's lap and she habitually stroked my forehead as we watched television together. Her gentle touch calmed my fears and anxiety. That specific childhood memory surprisingly flashed back several years after her death. The moment I recalled was while I was relaxing with my husband on the couch watching TV together. I laid my head back against his arm and he stroked my forehead several times the same way my mom used to. An over whelming feeling of grief shot through my body and I burst into tears as I stood in the middle of the den sobbing uncontrollably. He could not figure out what was happening and neither could I. The tremendous emotion I had bottled up inside came pouring out. Thoughts of her death caused the overwhelming sensation of emotion, I felt the final separation from her and deep sorrow in my spirit. Even though I had a husband and children of my own at that moment I felt totally abandoned. Remembering the heartache I caused my mother, remorse and guilt joined the tapes that harassed my thoughts.

George, a Sensitive, Caring Brother

My brother was born in 1934. Everyone called him Gigi, short for George I suppose. He was tall, thin and had sandy brown tightly curled hair and green eyes. He was a serious person and to me, he seemed to be nervous all the time; he bit his nails and laughed in short spurts when he saw or heard anything that made him laugh. After school, he helped repair cars in my dad's garage. When he turned sixteen, he bought a '51 Chevy convertible. He taught me how to start his car, put the convertible top down, and I felt special because he trusted me. He was a conservative driver, obeyed the rules of the road and I sat right next to him while he drove around to different places. Joey was the first of my brothers to join the military when he turned seventeen so I tagged along on Gig's dates. Friday nights we went to the movies. Admission for children was only eighteen cents. For a few cents more, I had enough candy to last all evening. The theatre offered a newsreel, a couple of cartoons, and double feature movie. After, he treated his date and me to a soda and something to eat at his favorite hangout, "The Hide Out."

Gigi was sensitive to my needs most of the time and knew I missed my mom a great deal. When he saw me crying for no reason, he would call her at work then drive me to the factory to see her. He would toot the horn, and she would peek out of one of the small windows and wave to us. To my surprise one evening, she was standing at the front door of the factory when we drove up and motioned to us to come in. I was eager to see what kept her away from home. She introduced some of her co-workers, and then brought us to the area where she worked. My mom operated a molding machine that made plastic products and was cooling a batch of Christmas ornaments she just removed from the machine. She handed me a little plastic icicle that glowed in the dark and I played with it all the way home. I liked my oldest brother because he was sensitive to my needs. He eventually joined the Air Force and I wrote to him often. To this day, I remember the serial number he was assigned. While stationed in New York, he met and married Margaret, my wonderful fun loving sister-in-law. I was thrilled when she asked me to be one of her bridesmaids. Her handsome brother Sonny was my partner walking down the aisle. Riding in the back seat with him, her other brother and his partner drove to the place where we were to take pictures, Sonny taught me how New York boys kiss. I will never forget him!

George was the child my mother had when she was nineteen. If one has the spiritual eyes to see God has a way to change tragedies into a triumph, George and Margaret had a daughter JoAnn, who inherited my mother's ability to sew, and is a buyer for a large department store; They also had two sons. Michael works with seriously troubled youth; David is deeply involved with the church, loves Jesus with all his heart, and has a Divinity degree. He has authored several books, written and published articles for magazines and counseled many men involved in the clean up after the attack on the Twin Towers in New York City.

Brother Joey, Fun and Heartache

My older brother was born in 1936. He was shorter than my other brother and had brown eyes and thick wavy brown hair. He was very smart and received good grades in school. He was extremely sensitive, had a great sense of humor and laughed hardily when something tickled him. As easily as he laughed, he could also cry spontaneously when saddened.

Joey was permissive when he babysat. I had no normal bedtime routine. He taught me how to whistle loudly using my fingers pressed to my lips a certain way. I learned a special code, he told me to listen for it while playing outdoors. Upon hearing his signal I had to whistle the code back so he knew I heard him; giving me just enough time to get home and jump under the covers before my mom came home from work. Half the time, he forgot to check to see if I did my homework. Often, I did not have time to wash up before I hopped into bed.

My brother received his driver's license when he was sixteen and bought a 1939 Plymouth with a rumble seat in the back. I tagged along with him and his friends when he babysat. He was not as conservative a driver as my oldest brother, and we went joy riding in his car frequently. Our favorite place was "roller coaster hill," where my aunt Ellie lived. The road was like no other around. It was steep and had three small humps twenty to thirty feet apart, called "Whoa Nellie's." My aunt told me the farmers traveling down that hill by wagon carrying vegetables, relied on those little humps to slow the wagon going down, otherwise the horse would be overtaken by the wagon. The road also had an S curve towards the bottom making the descending trip hazardous with horse and buggy. Anyway, my brother drove to the top, turned around and sped about forty miles per hour down the hill. When he drove over the "Whoa Nellie's" we'd fly off our seats, and roar with laughter.

My dad owned a Model T Ford he reconstructed into a truck, his pride and joy. He parked it across the street from our house and always carried the keys with him. Our parents went out one Sunday afternoon and Joey found my dad's keys on the kitchen table. We took the model T out for a spin. I loved the a-oo-ga sounding horn and we laughed hysterically together every time he tooted. As we drove around, I detected a snicker and glanced at him curiously. He had a smile on his face and his eyes were as big as saucers; his eyebrows were almost in his hairline. I could tell he was thinking of something more interesting to do. I think I figured it out as our eyes met for a quick second and we said in unison "roller coaster hill." He raced out into the country and up that infamous hill, then turned around and came speeding down. On the first bump, I flew off my seat and hit my head so hard the roof made a funny hollow sound. In our fit of laughter, my brother must have pushed on the gas pedal a little more forcefully because, as we drove over the third bump, the whole car flew off the road. A guardian angel must have been protecting us because we landed back on the road with all four tires intact. We were a little shaken not knowing what was going to happen then laughed all the way home. My dad never found out we had taken his Model T out.

Heartache and guilt resurfaced as I recalled an incident from my early teens. Joey joined the Army and spent most of his enlistment stationed in England. After his discharge from the service, he was not the same happy brother I knew before. The following Christmas my mom and dad decided to visit my brother Gigi in upstate New York. Joey stayed behind to take care of me. I had been dating someone and made plans to spend the holiday with my boyfriend and his family. I did not tell my brother, convinced he would not allow me go. When I heard my boyfriend's car in the driveway, I hastily blurted I was going to a friend's house for dinner threw my coat over my shoulders and stepped halfway out the door. As I pulled it shut, I heard him faintly ask me to stay home. Inconsiderate of his feelings I selfishly responded I did not want to, and closing the door, I heard him sob as it clicked shut. After my brother returned from the service he embraced a faith different from what we believed, and spent hours studying his Bibles. He no longer celebrated birthdays, Easter and Christmas. For many years, I thought I was responsible for his decision to follow another religion. Remembering the choice I made to leave him alone that Christmas, I wished I made the right choice instead. An emotion of sadness grips me spiritually each time I recall that incident.

Emotional traumas do influence the choices we make, making decisions right or wrong is the free choice we are given in life, and those decisions shape us into the people we become. Until we allow Jesus Christ to fill the "empty vacuum" in our heart we go on living life influenced by our learned behavior and spent emotions, reacting instead of responding to new traumas. All my wishing could not erase or change anything. My brother made his free choices for whatever reason he thought would work best for him. Internalizing truth from the Bible set me free from the emotional guilt I carried in my spirit. An intimate relationship with God through Jesus Christ as our Savior and Lord is the answer to heal our wounded emotions and stay on the course of God's plan for our lives.

Grandpa, a Sweet Tender Man

My grandfather was born in the late 1800's and lived in Hungary. His parents were God-fearing people and they attended a Reformed church. Marrying young, he and my grandmother came to the United States in 1904, settled in Bridgeport and lived in a boarding house for a few years. My grandpa' first job in this country was an iron molder. My grandparents converted to Baptist and joined the Hungarian Baptist church. He made a profession of faith was baptized, and attended prayer meetings and church faithfully every week. Having nine children in all, two years apart, they outgrew the house in Bridgeport, and then outgrew their home in the suburbs. He eventually bought farmland in the country and lived there until my grandmother died of a massive stroke in 1946. He moved to Wallingford and eventually married again.

Once a month on Sunday after church and dinner, we picked up one of my mom's sisters, and drove to Wallingford to visit my grandpa. He and my grandmother lived about an hour's drive from our house. Gramps was a short stocky man with neatly combed thinning silver hair on the top of his head, and he had a wiry short gray mustache. He always greeted me with a kiss and his mustache felt prickly on my cheek. As I recall he had big ears with hair growing out of them and thick bushy eyebrows. He also had a tender heart. In my eyes, his caring manner stood out more than his oddities. I loved to visit him because he took time to talk to me. His voice was raspy and he spoke in short sentences, and although he didn't laugh much, he had a funny laugh. He was a little hard to understand because he spoke a mixture of a little English and a little Hungarian. I chuckled when he tried to tell me stories. He often got impatient throwing his arms in the air in frustration because he couldn't think of the English word for what he

76

wanted to say. Other times he'd scratch his head and tilt it to the side, and look at me as if to say do you get what I am trying to say?

He and I walked and talked outside as we strolled along the path leading to the chicken coop and his flower garden. Occasionally, during our walks he would rest on one of the benches he had strategically placed along the path, and rub his "trick knee" as he described his arthritic knee. He said it would sometimes buckle beneath him, and he had to rest for a few moments before he could get up and walk again.

My grandpa was a Godly man who loved and worshipped the Lord. His Bible was dog-eared, well read, and he often left it open on the coffee table in their living room. My aunt Ellie told me several years after his death that he gave the Sunday sermon at church on occasion when the regular pastor was ill.

After our walk, grandpa excused himself and joined the conversation my grandmother, aunt and my mom were having in the kitchen. I sat in the living room listening to the murmur of their words in the Hungarian language as they conversed, and the ticking of the alarm clock my grandpa kept on the end table grew louder with the silence of the room. No negative tapes or voices bothered me when I visited my grandfather. I felt peaceful and calm inside.

Queenie

All my pets were another of God's unique life lesson plans to begin molding tenderness into my character. An unforgettable memory came to mind almost immediately after repeating the name of my very first pet, a beautiful long haired mixed breed part collie, part shepherd dog, Queenie. She followed me to elementary school one day and just before filing in the building, I told her to stay and wait. I forgot about her at the side door and rushed out the front entrance after school. Missing her at suppertime, I suddenly remembered where she was. Terror ran through my thoughts, fearing someone might have stolen her or she would get lost trying to find her way home; or worse hit by a car. I ran chastening myself all the way to school hoping to see her. There, she sat, panting, patiently waiting. I sobbed and buried my face in her fur as I hugged her tightly. Several years later, not realizing age was sneaking up on her, I became impatient when she did not respond quickly to my call, and impatiently kicked her. Despite my abuse, she continued to show her devotion to me. Near her sixteenth year, she disappeared one day. For several months I searched for her everyday. I thought how sorry I was for abusing her. I could not make up for my unkindness. She was a wonderful pet. It is through hindsight I see clearly even pets have a profound effect on our emotions and maturation process. Her loyalty and unconditional devotion eventually found a way to penetrate my hard heart. Patience and kindness were added to a growing list of character traits I have yet to learn.

My Playmates

I had many friends who were influential negatively and positively. I was what we called "tom boy" because I was rough and tough. Rita was quiet and shy. I envied her quiet, sweet and gentle spirit. Despite the many freckles on her face, she was a beautiful child. Her mom, dad, brother and little sister lived across the street. I could not understand why she couldn't play with us after school, when she could she had to watch her little sister, too. One day her little sister complained of a tummy ache. I remembered my mom used some smelly stuff she rubbed on her skin for her aches and pains so I ran home and got the tube of medicine. After I finished rubbing the cream all over her sister's stomach, she began screaming, "it burns, it burns." I sat at my computer emotionally reliving the panic I felt trying to feverishly wipe the cream off her sister's skin. Immediately following that episode, two vivid incidents I had completely forgotten involving her mom, dad and me broke through my thoughts and replayed in my mind. Realizing the severity of the memory, fear and anxiousness came over me like a dark cloud. I found myself wanting to go back in time to rescue my friend but I was decades too late. I sat there feeling dreadful, candidly reliving both troubling incidents in the present. Her mom and I were sitting on their front porch. She was rolling a little red colored bead in her hand and I curiously asked where she got it. I mimicked the area and pressed my finger to the corner of my eye and sure enough, a little bump about the size of the bead she was holding protruded from the corner of my eye. I tried to dislodge it several times and my eye became sore. I gave up thinking there was no way I could get it without hurting myself. On another occasion, I was standing near the bottom step to their porch waiting for my friend to come out and play; her dad sitting at the top step, called me closer to him. When I came within his reach, he extended his hand, and touched my private parts, starring hypnotically at me in the process. I still recall the black flashes in his eyes as I backed away from him. At that same moment, my girlfriend came bounding out of the house and we ran off to play. I totally forgot both incidents with her parents.

Bobby, the boy across the street was my one of my best friends. His parents were "down to earth" type people I liked both them both, especially his mom. She invited me in to have milk and cookies while I waited for Bobby to get dressed in the morning. His father worked at a local radio station and had all the latest hit records from the popular rock and roll stars of that time. Back in the 1950's, recorded music came on large vinyl discs. His dad made a record of his mom and him having a conversation, and played it on their record player for my mom and me. At my mom's request, he made a vinyl recording of her and me. In my mind, I can still replay the funny way I spoke, timidly pronouncing my words as I hesitated answering questions, having to repeat myself several times because I spoke too softly.

A low stonewall separated Bobby's yard from a small patch of woods and an open hay field where we played everyday. We dug a deep pit in the ground and lined it with hay from the field then broke branches from dead trees for the roof and laid them across the hole, leaving an opening at one end for an exit and entrance to our fort.

Bobby also taught me how to smoke when I was about ten years old. After school, we met at our secret place and smoked cigarettes he had taken from his parents' pack. My mom and dad smoked too, so I'd snitch a few when I could.

One chilly autumn evening after supper, we met at our fort, smoked the only cigarette he could get, then decided to light a little campfire to keep warm. Instead of digging a hole in the ground, we gathered up a few small stones and set them on top of the dry hay to contain the fire. I pulled some dead branches from the trees that were close by, picked up old newspapers that had blown into the field; he crumpled up the paper and arranged everything on top of the stones, then lit a match to it. As everything caught fire the wind stole some of the burning embers from the newspapers, and they sailed off into the air landing a short distance away igniting the dry hay. Unaware of what was happening only a few feet from us we sat warming ourselves in front of the fire, which also quickly spread out of control. We jumped up, ran to his house and watched the fire as it spread. One of the neighbors saw smoke coming from the open field and called the fire department. We never got caught.

I played touch football with another boy that lived across the street from me. I won most of the games and boasted winning. I didn't like being defeated when he won and threw temper tantrums. Amused at watching me loose my temper, he added more fuel to my out of control behavior by singing "temper, temper," laughing all the louder. I wasn't going to let him get away with making fun of me. He was strong but I managed to beat him up. I felt smug able to vindicate myself and get even. I stopped fighting when I realized someday I could get hurt, and used the power of not so nice words to lash back at anyone who made fun of me.

I stayed out late playing kick the can, hide and seek, and tag, until nine or ten o'clock with a few of the boys my own age. They didn't mess with me because they knew they would have to answer to my two older brothers. A new boy moved to the project and I quickly became infatuated with him. He was very cute, had blonde hair, freckles, big blue eyes, and two years older than me. I declared my love for him, and he in turn dared me to take my clothes off and put a pajama top on in front of him. I naively took him up on his dare; he kissed me then abruptly turned and ran away. I did not know why, perhaps he saw a neighbor or worse, one of my brothers. I did not realize he could have taken advantage of me sexually. I thought he saw something that was repulsive. Now I believe God put something in that boy's heart to make him run away. I did not know God existed back then.

Learning Life Skills -
Nothing Came Easy

Barbara lived a few houses down the street. I could not classify her as a playmate; she was more of an idol. She was tall, thin, had short blond hair, big blue eyes and three years older. I observed the way she took pride in her personal appearance, accomplished household chores, and concluded everything she did came out exactly right. I envied her beauty, the perfect way she performed her tasks, and tried copying her, but nothing I did turned out anything like the results she so effortlessly obtained. The harder I tried to copy her, the worse things turned out for me. One day after school, I watched as she set her hair with bobby pins. When she combed her hair out later, beautiful deep waves fell gracefully around her flawless face. I tried setting my hair the same way. When I took the bobby pins out and combed it, my hair stuck up everywhere and looked horrible. My thoughts dictated I could never be as pretty and smart, and do things as perfectly as she. Barbara had chores after school each day and I often sat and watched, between cleaning, she prepared dinner before her mom came home. I was envious of their relationship as I listened to their conversations, her mom spent time teaching her life skills, manners, how to cook and do the wash. My self-assessment dictated I didn't know how to do anything, but I was going to try to do something nice for my mom. Instead of going to her house after school one day, I decided to do something for my mom to help her. I was sure she would be proud if I proved I could help around the house. I changed into my play clothes and filled up our old-fashioned wringer washing machine, and proceeded to wash a load of colored clothes. There were blue jeans in that batch and when I tried to push them through the double rollers of the clothes wringer, water gushed and spurted from the jeans soaking the floor and me, the rollers of the wringer part of the washing machine then popped open. I had to tug hard to remove the massive piece of unyielding material from the vice grip like grasp of the rollers as they held the clothing fast between them. The jeans were still dripping wet so I put them through the wringer a second time, which popped the rollers open again. I struggled pulling the jeans through a second time. Hanging the clothes on the line outside was a lot easier than washing them and I was very tired when I finished but felt proud that I accomplished my task. I waited up until past eleven to tell my mom what I had done. She scolded me and said I was too young to use the washing machine. My mom had a friend with a deformed arm that hung limp at her side. To get her point across she told me my arm would be just like her friend's arm if the wringer caught hold of my hand. Emotionally disappointed, I couldn't understand the concern my mom tried to convey, or see the danger and consequences if my intended good deed went awry. I needed a more in-depth explanation, but my mom was not aware of that fact. Thoughts dictated I never could do anything right. I anticipated praise, received criticism and cried myself to sleep. My self-esteem plummeted.

Another embarrassing incident happened shortly after which affected my self -esteem again. My friend finished her chores and started making spaghetti sauce for dinner. Her mom walked in the door just in time to hear me exclaim how much I loved spaghetti. I watched her mom through the corner of my eye as she took off her coat and walked through their house checking to see if my friend had completed her chores then turned around and invited me to have dinner with them. I accepted and ran home, told my brother I was eating at my girlfriend's house and bounded in their door just as they were sitting down at the table. I sat in the empty chair. Her mom said something about piggish dirty hands, and curtly told me to wash. Neither of my brothers reminded me to wash before meals, most times I rushed in to supper, ate, then ran back out to play. The lesson in manners embarrassed me. I had more embarrassing lessons to learn that evening. My friend put the spaghetti noodles on the table and I helped myself to a large portion. I picked up a forkful and raised it as high as I could to get the end of the noodle in my mouth. My friend's mother sat with her eyebrows raised and asked rather curtly "Didn't anyone teach you how to eat spaghetti properly?" I received an earful about cleanliness, manners, and etiquette that night. I was at the age where even constructive criticism embarrassed me, I felt ashamed that I didn't know proper etiquette and I became overly sensitive about the way I ate. Negative tapes dictated I ate like a slob. I became self-conscious eating in front of anyone especially in front of peers at school. To avoid embarrassment, I ate my lunch with a few other girls in the girl's lavatory every day.

Sunday School

Saturday night when it was time for my weekly bath I had to pick a dress to wear so I wouldn't "dilly dally," as my mom used to say, on Sunday morning getting ready for church. I wasn't supervised, my mom told me to do a good job washing, but hardly ever checked after my bath. Typical of a child's behavior I put half an effort into washing, instead of scrubbing my body, I blew bubbles with the shampoo after lathering it on my hair, and played until my mom said it was time to get out of the tub. Personal hygiene didn't seem to be a high priority discipline. As a result, I was not "as clean as a whistle", even after taking a bath. Having poor personal hygiene, my peers avoided me. After my bath, I jumped into bed and snuggled under the covers to dry off. My mom set my brown shoulder-length hair with strips of rags. When she took them out in the morning, I had beautiful pipe curls.

All the Sunday school classes met as one unit, before we broke up into individual classes, to sing choruses and recite our weekly memory verse. I knew all the words to the songs and sang loud. In second grade I made a decision to be baptized with my class after making a statement of faith, but don't remember being immersed in the water. I'm sure I was though, we were members of a Baptist church. Each year we advanced to the next grade level. My Sunday school teachers had difficulty placing me in an appropriate class according to age because my birthday fell in January. I was too old for the young group and too young for the older group of kids and couldn't understand why they removed me from one class and stuck me in with younger children. I didn't fit in there either and felt like no one wanted me. The girls in my new class shunned me because I didn't dress the way they did and I acted goofy to cover up my insecure feelings. Preoccupied with how I looked, I believed my thoughts that kept telling me everyone had nicer clothes.

85

Even though my clothes were new, my thoughts convinced me that mine were not as nice as the clothes the other children wore. My mom purchased used shoes for me then painted them with shoe polish to look like "saddle shoes" which was the popular style then. That bothered me too, and my self-esteem whittled away little by little. I kept thinking I was odd. I believed that lie and as I got older, I wanted to stop going to Sunday school altogether but my mom said I had to, so I tried my best to behave and fit in.

Church

My mom and I attended church right after Sunday school and had a few minutes to wait before the church service began. My mom frequently chose to sit in the back; I slid in beside her then watched for a short, older Hungarian woman to enter the sanctuary. She usually dressed in a black outfit, toted a shiny black purse and wore a small black hat with a black veil that covered her face. Her routine was always the same, she came in, sat in the fifth row from the back, slid to the center, took a hanky out of her shiny black purse, and wiped her nose a few times. I chuckled to myself as I anticipated the routine reaction from the people already seated; listening for the "snap" her pocketbook made when she put her hankie away. It echoed through the sanctuary and everyone spontaneously turned to see where the noise came from. She wouldn't let anyone sit anywhere in that row. When someone tried to sit at the end of her row, she slid to that end and leaning into the person, gently pushed them out of their seat. I assumed they became embarrassed and rather than cause a scene, got up and found another. It was quite comical to watch at the time. Some reacted with surprise, others left mumbling something I couldn't understand, but everyone gave up their place when she slid close to them. I often wondered why she wouldn't allow anyone to sit in "her" row. Watching that elderly woman occupied my time as the pastor began the Hungarian segment of the service. Another thought that kept my mind busy was the way the women dressed for church, it seemed to me they tried to outdo each other. I had a vivid imagination when it came to making up conversations how one person would compliment the other saying..."Oh what a beautiful dress you have on and that mink stole, how lovely". I drew the conclusion that there was competition between them and couldn't understand the reason for it. They were there to worship I thought, or were they? I knew my mom and I were exempt because we had few new clothes compared to most of the women in church. Thoughts about different people kept me preoccupied as the speaker standing at the pulpit droned on in Hungarian. I tried my best to be quiet because I knew the children's story, although a brief ten minutes, was next.

Right on Target

I became aware of offending God with the wrong choices I made after hearing three stories the pastor told to the children. They reached their intended destination in my heart and made such an impact I never forgot them. One lesson was so profound I thought about it daily. The story was about a farmer who had acres of farmland, the richest soil, and grew the tastiest vegetables year after year; feeding his family and the entire town on the abundance of food from his garden. One day he woke up in a bad mood and went to work as usual on his farm. Something didn't go just the way he wanted it to and he swore for God to damn the thing that didn't go just right. God heard him and answered his hastily spoken plea. Everything in his garden withered. The farmer worked very hard but all his plants died, and for several years, nothing grew. His soil dried up and turned to dust. When he finally asked God why, God reminded him of his hastily spoken plea. God says," You shall not take the Name of the Lord Thy God in vain, for He will not hold him guiltless that takes His Name in vain. Exodus 20:7. The farmer told God that he was truly sorry and promised he would never take His Name in vain again, and asked to be forgiven for being so careless with his words. God forgave him and blessed his land once again, with an abundant harvest year after year. He thanked God for everything even when things didn't go right because he knew his Heavenly Father was in control of everything. The lesson I learned was God hears everything we say good or bad. I too, used God's name in vain so much it was a habit I wasn't even aware of until I heard that story. The lesson hit like a lightning bolt through my heart. I promised God I wouldn't take His name in vain anymore. Each time I slipped, I felt a tug on my heart, and became more aware of my offensive speech. I looked toward heaven and said I was sorry. When I repeated the offensive words again, negative thoughts in my head told me I was a failure because I wasn't able to keep the promise I made to stop.

During the special presentation time, people talked, passed notes, and rustled papers. Some snored while they slept, showing no respect for the person in the pulpit. One Sunday someone stopped in the middle of whatever they were doing and walked to the front of the platform, confronting the congregation of their rudeness and disrespect, then picked one of the people who was still carrying on and asked if they would like to take his place on the platform. The whole congregation came to attention, and the church grew so quiet you could hear a pin drop. I thought I'm glad they didn't pick on me! The person spoken to was embarrassed, but the incident served an unforgettable lesson that hit its mark in my heart. I thought if I were the person standing in front of everyone I'd want the congregation to be quiet and listen if not for interest then to show respect for the person standing behind the pulpit. From that day, there was a respectful quietness when the service began and continued throughout the Hungarian and English service, whether they were singing or preaching. Reflecting on that episode I'm sure the pastor had it staged, but then again people were quite different back when I was a child and I wouldn't put it past someone to have spontaneously reacted to the rude behavior displayed.

Exposed: A Childhood Secret

My mom's married sister, Ellie lived in a three-room apartment on the next street over the hill from where we lived in the project. Often she babysat me when my brothers couldn't. My cousin, who was two years younger, and I kept her busy playing mischievously together.

Aunt Ellie entered us in an Easter Parade contest at a nearby park. We marched in line with the other little girls dressed in new Easter outfits. A woman approached and asked what my name was. Broadly smiling, I answered through tightly stretched lips, distorting the sound of the letter B and pronounced my last name incorrectly. My mom asked why our last name was misspelled in the newspapers when she saw the article. I told her my smile was too big when the nice lady asked what my name was.

In my early fifties visiting my aunt Ellie in Florida after my uncle died, I decided to share an incident my cousin and I kept secret for years from childhood. First, I need to fill in some background information. I was about thirteen years old, my mom and I were driving on a two-lane road on our way to visit one of her sisters who lived in the country. I piped up, "I could drive this car with no problem." She replied, "oh yeah?" stopped the car, got out and told me to drive, calling my bluff. I was shocked and for a moment stared wide-eyed at her in disbelief. I was scared to death as we exchanged places, and I sat in the driver's seat. Our car was a 1947 Plymouth with a standard shift. I didn't realize how difficult it was to shift gears and had a hard time using the clutch in conjunction with the gas pedal shifting from one gear to another without making the car jump wildly. My mom did it so smoothly as I watched her shift the gears. I found out it wasn't that easy to drive, covered up my embarrassment by asking how to stop the stupid car from jerking then chuckled as I glanced over at her already in hysterics.

She encouraged me to try again. After a few tries I succeeded and she let me drive the rest of the way to my aunt's house.

Continuing the story I was sharing with my aunt Ellie; my mom and I drove to see the new house my uncle built for her sister in the country. I mused my mom named her road "roller coaster hill" and was the first one to speed over the three humps in the road as I described the long steep hill that twisted and turned on the way to her home. My aunt was going to a nearby orchard to get apples and invited us to go. I didn't want to, my cousin said she didn't want to either, so my aunt left my cousin in my care, and she and my mom took off leaving a car in the driveway with the keys in the ignition. We played in the drive-way for a few minutes then I remembered the keys in the car. I thought I'd make an impression and look grownup to my cousin if I showed her I could drive.

I told my cousin a short version of how my mom taught me to drive and asked if she wanted to go for a little ride up the road. She reluctantly agreed. We hopped in the car and I started it up. I never had an occasion to use the reverse gear before, but I remembered how my mom did it, and after I released the clutch, the car moved slowly backwards. Not looking to see if there was any traffic coming either way I stepped on the gas pedal and the car moved faster than I anticipated, at the end of the driveway I jerked the steering wheel a half turn and we wound up on the main road. There were no cars coming either way at the time, I believe because my guardian angel must have prepared the way that day. I shifted the gear into first and drove about a half mile. My cousin moaned the whole way down the road telling me to turn around, so I slowed down and attempted to make a U turn. The car almost stalled when I failed to push in the clutch but continued to move forward after I did. I tugged at the wheel to make the turn but didn't have enough room on the road to make it completely. Panic stricken, I pulled at the steering wheel a little bit more, forgot about keeping my foot on the clutch and the car stalled. We were stuck half on the grass and half on the road. I tried frantically to start the car and flooded it. As I tried again, the motor turned over. I shook uncontrollably and couldn't calm down, my legs jumped wildly as I pushed in the clutch to shift. I managed to get the car onto the road heading in the right direction, and reaching my aunt's house, pulled into the same spot it was parked in the driveway. We got out and rolled on the grass laughing and crying. I was shaking so much it was difficult to calm down. My cousin was angry and exclaimed she wouldn't ever do that again. We hadn't been back more than five minutes when my mom and aunt came home and asked what we had been up to while they were gone. Laughing, I responded, "Oh nothing, just playing here in the driveway". I got away with the lie. Years later, when confessing the story to my aunt she was speechless and sat with her eyes glued to mine. After about thirty seconds, she replied, "No you couldn't have", not believing I could do something like that. I smiled replying, "oh yes I did". I could tell she was at a loss for words by the way she squirmed in her chair, then turned and scolded me as if the incident had just occurred. By her reaction, I thought she would get up and swat me so I quickly responded "too late, too late". Whatever she was going to do next, she didn't. Instead, we both had a good laugh but I could tell from my aunt's reaction even then years later she didn't think it was as funny as I did.

School - The Best Years/The Worse Year

I liked gym class in elementary school. I held the longest record for being the fastest runner in relay races. I even dreamed about running. In my dreams, I'd start running from my friends' house and take one giant leap (about a hundred feet) landing in my front yard. I also dreamed I could fly. To gain altitude I had to hold my breath; making my body light enough to lift off the ground. The longer and deeper I held my breath the higher I rose, way above the treetops.

In school, I desired to please my teachers. I received good grades from kindergarten to fifth and obsessed to be first in spelling contests, I enjoyed winning and felt proud to be the best speller. English was my favorite subject; I loved to write essays. High grades came easy with very little study. I had no time for homework; I was too busy playing with my friends in the project after school.

My fifth grade teacher abruptly changed my study and homework habits. She gave lots of homework and demanded we do all of the work assigned. I feared her after seeing how she dealt with a student when he did not turn in his homework. I knuckled down, studied, and turned in all assignments.

My sixth grade teacher, a stern looking woman, did not smile, had an abrupt way of speaking and a gruff sounding voice. Her rules about class assignments and homework were simple to understand. She routinely wrote them on the blackboard, waited fifteen minutes, and then erased them. If we did not copy our assignments, we had to hunt down a classmate that did, and copy from them. She stated in the beginning of the school year she was not going to treat us like babies, we were old enough to be responsible to copy assignments on our own. As she called our name to bring our homework to her desk, she pulled out her grade book, announced our grade aloud, and recorded it in her book. Early on in the school year I happened to catch a glimpse of her talking to my fifth grade teacher one day in the hallway, the moment forever seared in my thoughts, she nodded in my direction and spoke softly out of the corner of her mouth, her lips hardly moving. Her eyes pierced right through me. Conferring with my fifth grade teacher, I am sure she learned I completed all homework assignments in fifth grade. I was capable of doing the same in sixth. I chose not to do homework, and my feeble excuses were unacceptable, she gave me a poor grade for work not done. She did not give second chances. My attitude changed, and for many years I blamed her for having a bad school year and a negative attitude towards school. I continued to attend because I had to, not because I wanted to.

Replacing false assumptions with truth, I realized I should have continued to apply the disciplines I learned. I needed to persevere, accept responsibility and continue to follow set guidelines; instead, I targeted my sixth grade teacher and blamed **her** for changing **my** attitude towards school. I suffered the consequences of poor decisions and became more insecure. If I made the right choice to discipline myself, I would have begun to develop a healthy feeling of self-esteem. I began to erect a wall in my spirit, strongholds of insecurity, fear, and anxiety confined emotions to my childhood preventing me from maturing emotionally. Stressful experiences, feelings of disappointment, abandonment, fear and anxiety created much chaos in my mind. I reacted by using antisocial behavior to override a poor self- image.

Poor Choices

Nearly failing sixth grade, I blamed the teacher instead of myself for poor grades and a negative attitude towards education, resulting in a rebellious attitude towards school and people in authority. To say it more plainly, I just did not care about anything or anyone but myself and made choices that were detrimental to my spirit, and emotional stability.

There were two popular social groups in my teenage years, "collegians," and "hoods". The collegians were kids that excelled in school. I chose to hang out with a small group of girls that identified themselves as " hoods". The six of us decided to establish a gang. Gangs were popular but not violent; they just got into mischievous trouble, mostly to the dismay of the teachers, principal and our parents.

Lung cancer not apparent to be a health hazard in the fifties, TV commercials and magazine articles glorified cigarette smoking and was becoming popular among the girls I associated with. Being an addicted smoker at ten years of age, when they began experimenting, I showed them how to inhale. Copying my example, I laughed watching them cough on the smoke, feeling superior.

Finding cigarettes in my jeans my mom confronted and threatened to burn my face if she ever caught me with a cigarette in my mouth before I could give her an explanation. Fearing she would carry through with the threat, I lied and exclaimed they were someone else's and she believed me.

The girls talked about going "all the way" with their boyfriends. I didn't know it was all talk and no action with them, but I believed every word they bragged. Having a desire to be part of the gang, along with my hormones being in high gear, I felt left out, I couldn't brag on that subject which seemed to be a daily discussion.

Just before my fifteenth birthday, on New Years Eve, one of the girls invited the five of us to her house for a party. Our boyfriends joined us after her parents were safely out of sight. We played rock 'n' roll music, danced and drank the liquor from her parents supply. My boy friend mixed a drink with orange juice and doubled the amount of vodka in each glass he made. I couldn't taste the vodka and downed several drinks while sitting in a rocking chair enjoying the music. Eventually I needed to use the bathroom and stood up. Numb and nauseous, I dropped to my knees and crawled to the toilet just in time to vomit what I thought was going to be my brains. I continued to drink on occasion when they did, but I did not like getting drunk.

Several months after the party I made a dreadful decision to give my virginity to a boy who said all the right words to convince me our love was going to last a lifetime together. We dated for two years, then, he broke up with me. I felt used and thrown away, but most significantly, deeply ashamed. I battled with low self-esteem listening to constant negative feedback in my thoughts. I could not reverse the physical loss I foolishly gave away and felt God would never forgive me for the poor choices I made. When I found out my friends lied about their sexual encounters, I became full of remorse and didn't trust anyone anymore. I suffered for many years the consequence of making a very poor decision just so I could identify with my peers.

In sixth grade, I met a girl who was different from the girls I knew before. She insisted we become blood sisters after we had been friends for a while. We vowed to always be best friends. We shared secrets, traded clothes, and slept over each other's house. We were fast friends for several years. My mom was grateful that I had a decent friend to pal around with and felt I was in good company knowing my friend's mom didn't work outside their home. I met boys I was interested in and smoked at her house; her mom never told mine. My friend introduced me to a fellow two years older and he visited me daily.

I skipped school more often than I attended and consequently failed my sophomore year. I decided to quit when I turned sixteen. My mother told me I would have to find a job and pay her rent. As an added incentive to stay in school, she stated my drivers' license was out of the question until I turned eighteen. I didn't care. I quit anyway, and got a job working in a department store.

My mom and I were getting our hair done by my aunt who did hairdressing in her home. Ever since quitting school, I felt confused and indecisive of my future. I would not admit I made a wrong choice to bail out on a free education, but one thing I knew for sure, I definitely did not want to continue working in a department store. My aunt encouraged me to pursue a Beauticians license. Encouraged by their counsel, even though I had to fund my tuition, I would not have to pay rent. Thankful, for the generous incentive, I enrolled. My mom chipped in and bought the text books required, and paid the fee for my state board exam. Receiving good grades gave me a sense of accomplishment. The State Board exam was difficult; in spite of making square waves with the Marcel iron, I received a passing grade on the written and practical tests and received my Hairdressers license in the mail six weeks later.

Shortly after passing the State Board exam, I turned eighteen. My dad made an appointment at the Motor Vehicle Department to take my drivers test. He knew most of the inspectors, and told me one his friends' would be testing my driving skills, but things did not turn out as planned. I wound up with a grumpy man who was very strict. In spite of mistakes, I passed. My dad allowed me drive the family car to work until I saved enough money to buy my own vehicle.

I continued to date the fellow I met at my girlfriend's house. Quite often, I smelled alcohol on his breath and did not have the good sense to break up at the first hint of a problem. The negative messages that played in my thoughts convinced me I did not deserve a better choice. Early on in our relationship, I made the mistake of telling him about my intimate relations with the fellow before him and he became persistent with me. I desperately wanted to fix the emotional pain of feeling "used" by my previous boyfriend, I reasoned if gave my body to this guy I could talk him into marrying me and marriage would fix the wrong choices I made.

We dated for a long time before I gained enough courage to introduce my boyfriend to my mother. She allowed him to pick me up at our home I didn't have to lie and sneak out anymore. We dated for another three years. In the beginning I hid my fear of getting pregnant when a certain time of the month rolled around. In time, my worried behavior became obvious to my mom and she began to suspect I was intimate with him. The following weekend my dad just happened to be home when my boyfriend came to call on me. Having a drinking problem when he was young, my dad detected an alcohol problem just by looking at him. My mom secretly arranged for me to spend the summer with her brother, at their cabin on a lake hoping the time away from each other would permanently separate us. Her plan did not work because I eventually called and gave my boyfriend directions to the lake. Motivated to fix the mistakes of my past, my mind focused on marriage, I started nagging him to marry me.

We dated a total of four years. I was nineteen going on twenty, he was twenty-two. We were old enough to make a permanent commitment. The idea of marriage did not excite him, he was getting what he wanted, but eventually I wore him down and he agreed. He could have easily walked away, why he did not I will never know.

He purchased a diamond ring and confided our plans to my aunt and uncle, they said we had to get my parent's permission. I called my mom and told her I was accepting a diamond ring from my boyfriend and hoped it was ok with her. She said NO! Not expecting her negative reply, I turned away from the others in the room and whispered hurtful words in retaliation. She reluctantly consented but asked me to wait until she could talk to me. I did not, and accepted the ring the moment I hung the phone up. My mom was so upset she made the half hour trip in record-breaking time and tried to convince me to give it back. I would not, no matter what she said. My stubborn will overrode any logic or sensible reasoning from my relatives or my mom. A day filled with gloom replaced a day meant for celebration, sealing the memory, forever regretting saying or doing anything to hurt my mom.

We planned our wedding in May on his birthday. At work I vomited every morning I was so nervous as time drew nearer, my boss suspected I was pregnant but time revealed I was not. We found a cute three-room apartment just before our wedding.

My dad stated he would never give me to an alcoholic. He did not attend my wedding! My oldest brother reluctantly walked me down the aisle. On our honeymoon, I learned just how much my husband drank, morning, noon and night. I did not know how he could consume large amounts of alcohol, vomit, and then, pour another as if he never got sick. The putrid odor made me vomit cleaning up after him. Living with an alcoholic husband was not a pleasant experience. Learning the hard way, I reaped the consequences of disobedience to my mom, dad and to God. The decision to marry to cover promiscuity only hurt me.

I stopped attending church. I felt terrible hurting my mom, to ease my guilty conscience, I set her hair every Saturday night. She listened as I vented problems. When it was time to leave, she never failed to invite me to go to church with her. I answered maybe, but really did not mean it.

My husband and I alternated visits to family on Sundays. His mom being curious to know if there was any prospect of grandchildren brought me to a fortuneteller after we were married a few years. I felt uneasiness in my spirit as the woman explained to my mother-in-law what she saw regarding future children.

We visited one of his married brothers in Rhode Island and spent the weekend. He and his brother drank constantly all day and night while they played cards, they passed out about two o'clock Sunday afternoon; my sister in law and I talked while they slept. When it was time to leave, he was still very much drunk. I debated whether to let him drive home. The front end of our car was severely out of line and shimmied when driven over fifty miles an hour. I was not an experienced driver, especially on the thruway, nor was I experienced to handle the handicapped car, but I believed that if I drove slowly, we would eventually arrive safely home. I slid behind the wheel with him asleep in the passengers seat and headed toward the entrance ramp, worked my way into traffic and stayed glued to the middle lane, hands tightly clutched on the steering wheel. Occasionally glancing in the rear view mirror, the car following appeared as though it was almost in our back seat. Traffic was heavy and cars sped past on both sides, drivers angrily tooted their horns and shook their fists in the air as they passed. Intimidated by the irate drivers I picked up speed, the car started shaking so violently I had difficulty keeping the steering wheel steady; pulled to the side of the highway and stopped. Terrified to go any further, I woke him up after remembering he never got into an accident while driving drunk and presumed he drove well drunk or sober. Feeling a positive affirmation in my thoughts I asked him to drive. I made a very bad decision. He got into the drivers seat and stomped on the gas pedal recklessly taking off into the traffic. I sat in the passengers seat with my teeth clenched all the way home as he drove one hundred miles an hour weaving in and out traffic. I cannot believe every state trooper was somewhere else on the road that day. We arrived safely home, but it took quite a while to calm down from the horrendous ordeal. Reliving that episode, I knew God's Hand of protection kept us safe, but I was not aware of His presence then.

If You Can't Lick 'Em, Join "Em

The old saying is if you can't lick them, join them, so I decided to drink along with him. People looked carefree when they drank. I thought drinking would help me forget my problems. The alcohol had the opposite effect. Feeling deep remorse from acts of unkindness, I relived painful experiences and deep overwhelming sorrow from disobedience to my parents. One sobering thought kept running through my mind, my mom and dad were right when they advised me not to marry him but I chose to go my own stubborn way, and I suffered the consequences of making another dreadfully wrong decision again.

At work, I began to see my co-workers work ethics as cutthroat competitors. I decided that hairdressing was not for me. Greatly disillusioned, I concluded people cared more about money and vanity than helping each other succeed. I floundered trying to find happiness; instead, life dealt one disappointment after another. In my spirit, I began ever so slowly to disconnect from the world around me.

I applied for factory work at a nearby aircraft plant, doing subassemblies for helicopters and discovered I loved working with power tools and became so proficient filling work orders; my boss transferred the two other women in my department to a different section of the plant. Nicknamed "twenty minutes" I assembled any part requested in twenty minutes or less.

The fellow in the next department was cute and we flirted back and forth. He never mentioned his wife or the fact that she was in her last few months of pregnancy. Unhappy in my marriage; the flirting grew serious on my part. We met at a near by park few times after work. On evening, I invited him to my apartment. I believe he had second thoughts about his marriage and left apologizing. I tried to see him a few times after that but somehow all my attempts were blocked.

Baby Steps:
Aroused By Holy Gentle Tugging

I began to feel a strong conviction in my heart that what I did was wrong remembering the definition of adultery from a sermon at church. Confronted with truth, I was guilty the moment I started flirting and the burden of my shameful conduct was ever present in my thoughts. I could not run away from problems by drinking nor could I silence harassing thoughts. Alcohol did not absolve shame or take away past painful experiences. Overwhelmed from guilt, my moms' invitation to attend church with her popped into my mind. Perhaps there I could confess my sin to God and find relief from the heavy weight of sin I carried in my spirit. The following Sunday I slipped into the pew and sat down beside my mother. I thought she was going to faint right there on the spot. I bowed my head and told God how truly sorry I was about my infidelity. I did not know whether He heard me or not nor did I know whether He would ever forgive me, but I begged repeatedly for forgiveness. When I looked up from my prayer my mom was crying and she continued to cry all through most of the service. I decided if God was to ever forgive me I should start going to church regularly.

I became aware of a still small voice prodding me to think about the places I frequented with my husband, and this strong inner desire to change, to make things right, to feel better about myself. One evening while sitting at the bar with my husband, after going to church that morning, something inside said I was living a double standard, going to church in the morning and sitting in a bar at night. I thought about my marriage, the future, and the direction my life was going discouraged I could not persuade my husband to stop drinking. The next day I packed my clothes and left, but felt overwhelmingly insecure, and returned to our little apartment before he even knew what I had done. Emotionally troubled I put my things away then turned on some instrumental mood music and thought about our lives again. He drinks too much, he drinks first thing in the morning, that is not normal I told myself, one thought leading to another. I recalled a conversation with his dad who was also an alcoholic, he confided he introduced all four of his sons to alcohol when they were in their early teens, and was quite proud he had drinking buddies in his own family. It did not register then, now realizing I was trying to win a loosing battle. In my need to cover mistakes of the past, I denied the truth that I married for all the wrong reasons and made poor choices. Consequently, I was stuck in a marriage with a man that had a colossal problem. He was a full-fledged alcoholic and needed to acknowledge his dependence, but he was not ready to do that.

The private yacht club we were members of threw a big New Years Eve party and we attended every year for the four years of our marriage. I would always save a dance for his dad. I thought he was a big old teddy bear even though I didn't like his drinking. By evening's end, I would have a different opinion of my father-in-law. My husband's parents had just celebrated their twenty fifth wedding anniversary, and extended their celebration to the New Year's party. From my point of view, they looked like the perfect couple and kept perfectly in step with each other. We were dancing to a slow song and came within earshot of his mom and dad on the dance floor. I overheard his dad whisper to my mother-in-law that he would like to put his shoes under the bed of the redhead dancing with her husband across the dance floor! I wondered how my father-in-law could be so thoughtless and cruel to make that hurtful comment to the wonderful woman he was married to for so many years. I had no idea whose still small voice it was that spoke again to my heart at that moment but I distinctly remember; like father like son, is that where I wanted to be twenty-five years from now? I thought about his drinking, our marriage and questioned what I wanted out of our marriage. I hated living with an alcoholic. The good I wanted had a tug of war with what I lived with and a continual battle for a more secure way of life began to sway my thinking.

The next day I approached my husband again when he was a little more sober and asked him to stop drinking, threatening to leave if he wouldn't. He promised he would stop and agreed to counsel with the pastor of the church where we were married. He called me from his favorite bar a few days later and told me he stopped to play a game of pool with his brother and dad. When I asked if he had been drinking he answered he was drinking club soda. I gave him the benefit of the doubt, and trusted that he told me the truth. Eventually I smelled liquor on his breath, I expressed my disappointment and hurt. Another broken promise was all I could say, and headed for the den, my little sanctuary, where I emotionally escaped my unpleasant marriage.

I phoned my dad's youngest sister, as I did many times when in need of positive feedback to problems, only this time I looked-for encouragement to leave my husband. Hearing constant complaints about how unhappy I was she bluntly told me to live with his drinking or leave him. Surprised at her answer, I knew I could not go on living with his drinking and broken promises. Looking for love outside of my marriage also made me realize I should not stay in a relationship I could not honor. The next time he came home drunk I declared I was tired of his drunkenness, broken promises and was going to divorce him. Infuriated, he raised his hand and it connected to my mouth splitting my lip; then turned and ran out of the house. A few days later, I returned to pick up several of my belongings and found our apartment empty. My clothes were gone; the furniture I charged on my credit was gone. The shock of finding an empty house unearthed the trauma of childhood abandonment and imprinted the memory deeper into my subconscious mind. I began building a sturdy wall around my emotions to protect my fragile feelings. I became overly protective of things I owned and mistrusted everyone, even people that were closest to me.

Anxiety, fears, guilt, shame, loneliness, and abandonment, wove their roots deeply in my hurting heart, had free reign in my thoughts, and reappeared at stressful, vulnerable times throughout my life.

Yielding To Holy Gentle Tugging

Offenses to God and the people I loved, replayed repeatedly in my mind. Infidelity continued to burden my spirit. To cope I stuffed feelings in my heart and put on a happy face in front of others, but when alone, I deeply agonized the degrading consequences of poor choices, feeling unloved and abandoned, with childlike emotions.

Comforted to be with my mom again, I started going to church with her. I became aware of a gentle tugging at my heartstrings, something was slowly happening in my spirit. I became more appreciative of my mother. We talked more about life situations. She asked me to obtain my high school equivalency. She insisted, I believe, not wanting me to make the same mistakes as she. I promised I would some day soon. Little did I know cancer was internally ravaging her body and I had a short precious time left with her.

We visited one of her sisters after church, as we so often did when I was a young girl. I especially liked my mom's youngest sister Ellie because she had a great sense of humor. I also sensed her genuine concern when I confided not knowing how to resolve many hurts and unanswered questions. Auntie Ellie told me her pastor counseled people contemplating and going through divorce. She encouraged me to make an appointment. Wednesday night prayer meeting would be the soonest I could see him, three days to wait.

Wednesday night I visited her church and bravely sat down among the people already gathered. I was most always intimidated to venture out on my own and didn't know where the boldness came from to even enter a prayer meeting. One by one people introduced themselves, I acknowledged their friendliness but felt conspicuous, out of place. After the meeting I approached the pastor, gave him a brief explanation of why I was there and asked if he could help me. He smiled said he could, and set a date for an appointment the following week. The days dragged as I rehearsed what I was going to say regarding my marriage.

Invited into the pastor's office, my palms were sweaty as I nervously turned the doorknob. The first sentence I blurted were my plans to go through with my divorce and nothing he could say or do would convince me otherwise, then introduced myself and sat down. I glanced into his eyes and did not see any condemning look on his face. He made no comments about what I should or should not do. I mentioned my aunt Ellie's suggestion to make the appointment to see him. He asked about my parents, and family. We talked about my husband. I felt comfortable as we conversed and told him the whole sordid story, including the affair I had. He listened intently. When I finished, he asked if I owned a Bible. After acknowledging that I did, he gave me homework. He asked me to say a prayer before reading I Corinthians chapter seven, then ask God to speak to me regarding my decision to divorce my husband. We prayed together and I left eager to read what he asked.

I got home and impatiently looked for my Bible. I was not an avid reader and it took me quite a while to find the verses. The Bible said... no... God said, I had no spiritual grounds for divorce. Disappointment crushed any hope of making the right decision. Stubbornly determined to carry out my plan, no matter what consequences came with the decision, the next time the pastor and I met I told him what I thought the scripture said, but nothing was going to stop me from my plotted course. I wanted to change my life, and earnestly did not want to continue living a life of church in the morning and a tavern at night. I wanted to help people get to know God. He suggested I attend a "Lay Institute for Evangelism" seminar with a group from his church. I thought about it for a few days and decided to go. I needed to learn how to tell others about God. Little did I know that seminar would change my life forever.

Choices Based on Emotional Needs

Our day in court arrived and I met with my lawyer in a little room just outside the courtroom. My husband was there with his lawyer. He pleaded with me not to go through with the divorce but I knew I could not live with his drinking problem. I told him I hated his drinking and did not like taverns, and felt uneasy around drunken men. Besides, he could not guarantee me that he would ever stop drinking. I wanted to live a more decent life. I wanted God in my life more. I wanted to put the past behind me and start over. He had nothing to say.

We went into the courtroom and waited. Fear numbed my minds, our case was called and I repeated the oath to tell the truth, the whole truth with my hand on the Holy Bible. I said a silent prayer to God that whatever happened was His will for my life. The judge asked my name; my mind went blank. It seemed like an eternity before I could think of something to say. I hastily stated my first name, then asked myself, should I say, my maiden name or my married name? Who was I? After a long pause, I stated my married name. The judge then asked why I should be granted a divorce. Again, my mind went blank. The only thing I thought of was that frightful experience driving home one hundred miles an hour with my husband drunk at the wheel and blurted the whole story out to him. After my testimony, he paused, looking at me over the rim of his glasses, and granted the divorce. I made a request to have my maiden name reinstated and asked the judge if he could do that. He could, and did.

The Best Decision I Ever Made

The "Lay Institute For Evangelism" seminar I signed up for arrived a few weeks after my divorce. I met the group of men and women in the church parking lot. When all arrived, we boarded the waiting van and were soon on our way to the meeting. I was excited. I was going to learn how to tell people about God and start a new life. We parked a few blocks from the building and chatted with each other as we walked. We filed into a dull-lit hallway, made our way to the room and then stood waiting to sit. The people leading the seminar introduced themselves and one person from the group gave an introductory speech. I didn't understand what they were saying. After the person finished giving a brief explanation of what they hoped to accomplish, we were asked to form a single line and count off by two's then sit with our partner at a table.

I felt nervous and uncomfortable but complied. A very nice woman was my partner. We sat across from each other, exchanged names, but I was so nervous I did not remember hers. The instructor gave each of us a little pamphlet of "*The Four Spiritual Laws.*" They told us to turn to the page that read, "**God loves you and has a plan for your life.**" We did. We were instructed to say it with expression: "*God really does love you and has a plan for your life.*" I repeated it first, my partner followed. The woman in charge told us it was a good attempt, but not convincing enough. She told us to say it again with more confidence. We went through it again, first my partner, then me. I guessed we weren't really getting it right because our instructor announced that we needed to repeat it with more feeling and this time to say the words as if they were the last we would ever say to each other. When my partner said, **ROSEMARY, GOD LOVES YOU, HE LOVES YOU,** the words penetrated through my blinded spirit and something wonderful happened. The Holy Spirit quickened my spirit, as though a light bulb turned on in my brain and in that moment I knew that I knew that I knew **GOD LOVES ME, HE LOVES ME!** God's Spirit had penetrated my heart. Something also very significant happened at that very moment. I remembered some of the people from my past who witnessed to me about Jesus. The pastor who gave the children's sermons at my church when I was little, one of my Sunday school teachers, and a woman I briefly worked with in a shoe store. It was such a memorable experience I never forgot it. We went through the rest of the *Four Spiritual Laws* that evening and I invited Jesus to forgive my sins and to live in my heart. forever. The guilt and shame I carried was gone. I felt freedom in my spirit that I never felt before. I danced all the way up the sidewalk on the way to the van and told everyone that I gave my heart to Jesus. I stopped at a trash container, reached into my jacket pocket, and threw away the new pack of cigarettes I purchased earlier that day. Giving my heart to Jesus that evening was the best choice I ever made. I was so overwhelmingly grateful that He could love a sinner like me. As we rode home, I wondered if my partner knew she led me to salvation that evening.

Waking up the next morning, I looked out the window at the world outside. The landscape was the same as the day before but the natural beauty of nature seemed to pop out everywhere. Everything I observed had depth and meaning, and life felt wonderful as I experienced the "new life" God promised in the Bible. His Holy Spirit was alive in me!! I basked in God's love and the beauty of His creation as I stood gazing out my window.

It was Monday morning. I went to work a changed person. I had a hunger and thirst to read God's Word and grasped my Bible on my way out the door. I read it during lunch. I habitually grabbed for my pack of cigarettes when I went to the restroom, then remembered I quit smoking, shrugged off the gesture and continued on my way. I smoked two packs of unfiltered cigarettes a day since my teens and should have experienced some kind of withdrawal symptoms. I believe God healed me from my addiction and I never once experienced withdrawal from tobacco.

Everyone at work noticed the change right away and when I read my Bible at lunch, co-workers ridiculed me. Rosie has religion they taunted. In my spirit, for the first time I could sense heavy oppression, a very uncomfortable feeling, but I also knew I had something more wonderful. I did my work and talked to people about Jesus whenever the opportunity arose.

I started attending the Baptist church and joined their choir. One of the women I enjoyed being with was a wonderful caring Christian. I liked her right from the moment we met and felt a kinship to her because she was from Hungarian decent, and so was I. Dottie encouraged me in my new faith and invited me to call if I needed help understanding the Bible; I called often. She offered an invitation to have lunch a few months later, and I accepted. I shared my feeling of oppression at work and at home. My parents did not understand the enthusiasm I openly expressed about my faith in Jesus. Years ago my older brother displayed a similar enthusiasm but our beliefs were vastly different. My dad I guess was an atheist, my mom feared I would follow my brother's footsteps, upset with what he believed and outwardly practiced. Dottie invited me to move in with her family for a while if I needed to get away. I decided to make that move because I was not growing spiritually living with my parents.

My friend and her husband had five children and lived in a lovely Cape Cod style home. They also cared for two children whose father had recently gone through a divorce. I stayed with my new adopted family for just a brief period, and found living in a Christian home was so different from what I experienced in my home. I observed a home filled with interaction, respect and love between all who lived there. Dottie's husband Everett was head of their home; he also had a personal relationship with Jesus that showed in his actions as well as his words. He was kind and gentle, yet firm when he needed to be, and answered all of my questions using his Bible as he gave explanations. I confided that I was lonely but because of the deep wounds from my past, I was afraid to get serious with anyone. Everett was kind and loving, I thought if I ever met anyone he would have to be just like him. Dottie was also kind and loving, tempered with just the right amount of discipline, and a whole lot of energy. The two children staying there called her "mommy Hallquist." She was a fantastic mother. I could plainly see her children loved their parents. There was no shame, and disagreements resolved with discussions between husband and wife. They spoke lovingly and showed affection to each other often. We attended church together on Sunday, and Wednesday nights we went to Bible study/prayer meeting. One Sunday after church, my aunt Ellie met me in the parking lot and scolded me for moving out of my parent's home. I tried to explain but she cut me short stating my mom's doctor found a cancerous growth, she was to have immediate surgery, and she needed me then strongly suggested I move back home where I belonged. That Sunday I packed up and moved back to my parent's house. My mom had her operation the day after Mother's Day. The doctor removed her breast and said the cancer had already spread to the lymph nodes under her arm but he assured me he removed all the cancer he saw. Not having medical knowledge especially about cancer, I did not know what he meant by that statement. She went through Chemotherapy and the treatments made her very sick. After what seemed like forever she regained much of her strength, was able to drive her car again and tried to carry on her normal routine. Even so I wondered what was going to happen to her. Living home wasn't easy and I found trying to live my new faith very difficult. My mom thought I prayed and read my Bible too much, my dad said unkind things about Jesus, and it hurt my heart to hear God's Name taken in vain. I thought things would be different with the threat of cancer and the emergency surgery my mom went through but my parents continued to argue and say unkind things to each other. I wished they would show affection to each other instead of silence or hateful words. I wanted them to love each other.

A Subtle Deception

I let my spiritual guard down a little more each day living at home unaware of what was happening in my spirit. Insecurities slithered in one by one; I had not processed fears and anxieties from my past that imprisoned my thoughts. Deep seated rejection and abandonment, problems from my childhood and rejections I experienced as a child and in my adult years needed to be processed. I needed intense counseling. On the surface, I thought everything was going great; subtly fooled into believing that Christ was on the throne of my heart.

Dottie invited me for lunch again. I arrived early and observed the children's father playing with them. She introduced him. He spoke abruptly. I did not like that characteristic; it reminded me of my sixth grade teacher. I felt uncomfortable in his presence, yet I felt attracted because I knew he was born again too. We talked briefly and I met his two children. The boy warmed up to me right away but the girl was cold and indifferent. I tried several times to get a smile out of her, but she held a staunch stiff stance wanting nothing to do with me. We spent a few more minutes chatting together then he excused himself stating that he had to get ready for work. I felt confident he would call for a date.

Weeks passed. Loneliness became unbearable and he monopolized my thoughts. In my younger years, boys jumped at the opportunity to date me. I phoned him. He informed me that he worked swing shift at the police department and was either working or sleeping, he had very little social time. He had been dating someone for several months; her parents encouraged her to break off their relationship when they learned that he had two children. I presumed that if I were to pursue a relationship with him I would also have to accept them. I encouraged him by saying I wanted to get to know his children better. We dated for a few months then he invited me to the Policemen's Ball. My mom and I shopped in New York for a dress. Having little confidence in my intelligence, I relied heavily on my looks to keep him interested.

We were like two geese that could not fly at the ball. We didn't smoke, didn't drink and couldn't dance with each other. He asked if I was enjoying myself and I said no, neither of us were party animals. We left the dance and he drove me home. Parked in my driveway, we sat in the car and talked. I felt comfortable with him; he did not try to take advantage of me on our first date. Obsession held me fast and I thought about him constantly. I met and liked his mom and dad. My parents were more reluctant because of his two children, but after a few conversations with him, they felt at ease knowing I was dating a decent fellow.

My attraction grew steadily stronger and I desired to be part of his life. He made me feel important, attractive and needed. I had a false idea that my (future) husband was going to meet all my needs; he would always be there for me. I shifted responsibility for my happiness to my (future) husband. Wrong reasoning, he could never measure up to all my expectations.

Impulsive Commitment

We dated just six months then made plans to take the plunge into marriage in the fall. A few weeks before the date we set to tie the knot, he mentioned feeling unsure of his decision to marry me. Creatively I convinced him otherwise. Looking back, I realized I shouldn't have.

Let me clarify that issues and incidents are from my perspective, my point of view. He had pluses and minuses in his life just as I did but I can only relate to mine. They say opposites attract, and boy, were we opposites! Even so, looking back I gleaned and grew more from our twenty years of marriage.

We were married in October seven PM on a Friday evening in our pastor's home. My mom, dad, and grandfather were present as well as his mom, dad and two children. Dottie and Everett stood with us to witness our marriage, and all five of their children attended.

Everett possessed a contracting business and owned a house next to his office in the center of town several miles away and offered to rent it to us. We accepted. He also offered my husband a job doing carpentry after hearing he wanted to quit the police force. My hubby received his degree in carpentry, but hardly used his skill. He chose to be a police officer instead.

His children began calling me mommy from the minute we said, "I do", something I had to get used to rather quickly. With everyone's blessing and the generosity of Dottie and Everett renting a trailer for us, we were off to spend our two-week honeymoon in the Blue Ridge and Shenandoah Mountains.

Mid fall was most beautiful that year and the rapidly changing season waited for us as we headed south with trailer in tow. Approaching each quaint little town we were awestruck at the brilliant hues of red, orange and yellow leaves that hung in place on each stately tree proudly displaying their vibrant colors. Gorgeous weather also accompanied us. The days were warm and sunny through most of our honeymoon. We had fun together and enjoyed the points of interest in each state we visited. As we drove, the beautiful colored leaves, so picturesque on the trees as they waited our arrival fell to the ground as we departed and the season abruptly changed to bareness, anticipating winter's arrival.

The road was narrow and windy leading up the Blue Ridge Mountains. There were no guardrails along the right side of the road; I got sick to my stomach looking down into the valley below, hundreds of feet to the bottom. Nightmares invaded my dreams for the first few nights, but by the time we reached the summit, they disappeared.

Nights were somewhat cool and the clean crisp mountain air was refreshing to breath. We hiked to Clingman's Dome, took pictures then headed back to our trailer. On the way, we kept seeing signs that read BEWARE OF THE BEARS. What bears? I thought. So far, we had not seen any. Rounding a bend we encountered a car in the middle of the road and thought it odd that the driver parked there. We pulled along side slightly ahead and looked to see if the driver was ok. Still in his car, he signaled to us pointing to the left side of the road. Then we saw it, a big black bear sitting by the roadside. My husband wanted to snap a picture of it so he grabbed his camera, got out of the car and walked slowly up to what looked to me like an eye-to-eye shot of the bear. When he reached about fifteen feet of the beast I shouted to him after noticing the animal's ears sharply turn toward the back of its head as it slowly stood up and moved toward my husband. I shouted "run, run, get back to the car," he insisted on taking the picture first, and he did, then he ran. I held the door and he jumped in and quickly pulled the door closed just in time, thank God. When we got the film developed there was one picture with a faint blur of something black. We figured that must have been the one he took of the bear, and both had a good laugh.

I enjoyed trailer camping, it was my first; though not a true "roughing it" camping experience, but not my last. We had such a tiny trailer there was no place for personal privacy. At first, I was embarrassed but he made me feel special and comfortable. We prayed and read our Bible together at the beginning and end of each day. As we prayed, I became aware that we were opposites. He was very intense, regimentally systematic and had a plan for everything. I was happy go lucky, giddy, and undisciplined. I did things as the mood struck me most of the time. I was also very emotional and tears came readily, births, happy and sad events, death, baby christenings, weddings, funerals, and songs both spiritual and secular set me off on crying spurts when the emotion hit me. It was hard for him to find humor in anything and I learned later that he found it difficult to laugh at his own mistakes. I figured God put us together because we were the missing link to each other. What he lacked I had and vise versa. Together we would grow to become of like mind through the years each filling in that missing part of our lives making us what God intended us to be, if we kept God in our lives. When we prayed together aloud we saw through the eyes of each other how we interpreted life situations and people around us. We also learned that there was more than one way to perceive a situation. I knew in my heart that as long as we kept God first in our lives and first in our marriage, that He would bless us. Praying together united us spiritually.

We reached our destination near the top of the mountain and chose a campsite in the state forest. God allowed me to see a glimpse of my husband's temper when he lost it trying to back our little trailer into a parking space. He rested from the days driving and the wild encounter with he bear, while I made supper.

Glancing out of the tiny window, I commented how beautiful the evening sky looked. Brighter than previous early evenings, we stepped out of our tiny shelter to investigate. Looking toward the heavens, we saw the most beautiful display of colors filtering through the trees. The sky was aglow with dazzling hues of red, pink, blue, gray, purple and white as we caught the sun setting. Wanting to capture this magnificent sunset on film, we hopped in the car and drove until we could drive no further toward the top of the mountain. We found a clearing and he snapped a shot of the most beautiful sunset we had ever seen. Although the picture did not come out as we personally experienced it, the magnificent panorama God created for our eyes was such a wondrous gift, I never forgot the beauty of it. God revealed His awesome majestic power and control of nature in the most glorious sunset we would probably never see again. I felt as though God wrapped His arms around and blessed us at that moment. God continued to bless with breathtaking scenery as we journeyed through the mountains, enjoying every day of our honeymoon.

Driving home, I thought about what family life would be like with his children living with us. Insecure thoughts dictated if I did not measure up to what he expected he would surely leave me so I made a mental note of the things he did not approve of before we married, and made sure I would not intentionally do those things. I made a mental note too, of his favorite colors, food, interests, hobbies, TV shows, and music. He asked specifically if I knew how to bake, and if I did any preserving or canned any vegetables. I thought about my aunt Ellie, who had a large vegetable garden, and all the work she did preparing for her harvest in the fall; sterilizing jars, cleaning, cutting up, cooking and filling those jars with vegetables and fruit. Too much work, I said aloud, grocery stores had good food. After those words came out of my mouth, I worried that he would think I was lazy.

Instant Motherhood - A Wake Up Call

Returning from our fabulous honeymoon, we picked the children up and plunged into life together as a family. God blessed me with a wonderful Christian husband, and two small children to love and care for. I naively imagined the children were going to be well behaved and obedient. I was also on a quest to prove to those who doubted our second marriage would last that ours would be successful; trials and hardships I planned to meet with faith, perseverance, and hard work.

Unaware of subconscious insecurities, lack of confidence showed its ugly head first. Reminiscing bits of our conversations dating, somehow I came away feeling I had to measure up to my husband's expectations, so the goals I set were extreme. I burned our first evening meal together. I did not have time to prepare another so I frantically tried to salvage enough food to feed everyone. I cooked delicious meals in my first marriage, and could not understand why I made mistakes now. To save my injured ego, I thought of a clever way to cover up the disaster, and we ate by candlelight. He did not complain; surprisingly he found something to compliment and always thanked me after every meal. The more he complimented, the more I desired to please him. Perhaps I tried too hard to make a good impression. The truth was, mental preoccupation of incompetence prevented successful efforts.

Our apartment was located near a train station. In fact, we lived three houses away from the railroad tracks. Each day the train zoomed by and everything in the house shook. A few months later, we hardly noticed it.

The children never failed to spill their cereal and or glass of milk at breakfast. They had poor eating habits and I was not used to the mess they made, unaware all children were messy. After breakfast, I washed their face and hands and sent them in the back yard to play in the large

118

fenced in parking lot. Confident they would obey I told them not to go near the fence, kept the back door opened, and visually checked frequently. Interrupted from mopping the floor by a knock on the screen door, Everett stood on the back steps with a child under each arm he rescued from the railroad tracks. My thoughts immediately focused on the express train that thundered past the tiny railroad station several times a day, and feared my husband would be angry for not supervising them personally.

My in-laws lived in a cute cape cod style home about ten miles away. I don't know what they thought when they heard about the children being rescued but shortly after the incident, they insisted we move in with them. His parents purchased a home in Florida and planned to retire there in six months. My husband was quick to make an affirmative decision to move. I surmised they thought I was incompetent to keep their grandchildren safe.

Winter arrived, my husband complained that he did not like working in the cold, and wanted to change his occupation. We made it a nightly prayer request God would make a way to provide the funds for schooling, food and doctor bills if it was His will. Amazingly, God answered that prayer sooner than we anticipated. My husband received a scholarship from the State of Connecticut to study teaching. God provided medical assistance from the state for the children; the government extended the GI Bill to include men who fought in the Cuban conflict, which included him, for books and money to live on. Living sacrificially was a humbling experience, but God met all our needs. We were married only four months when I got pregnant. I was elated, my husband was happy too.

Stress - the Catalyst to Insecure Thoughts

Packing to move negative thoughts replayed repeatedly. I worried about my inexperienced mothering skills and felt stupid for not possessing the common sense to supervise outdoor playtime with my newly acquired charges.

Preparing meals, I switched dishes, pots, pans and food around to my convenience. His mom was normally a very soft-spoken woman, but when she came home that evening and found everything in the kitchen rearranged she angrily exclaimed we were living in her home and she did not want her things changed around until they departed for Florida. I hated myself for upsetting her I did not know how to fix her angry feelings. Her angry words played repeatedly in my mind.

The children bickered with each other during their play. I strived to be a good mom and tried to resolve their conflicts instead of letting them resolve disputes on their own. Listening to each of their excuses, I could not discern which one started the spat, nor did I know whose side to take adding more stress to my already over burdened emotions. Perhaps they acted out to get even with me, I thought. My husband assured me they were only being children, but I did not believe him.

Weekdays I packed a lunch with a love note tucked in for my husband, and sent him off to work. I had no idea before we married both children were bed wetters. Waking them in the middle of the night did not help; many instances they were already wet, other times they wet a second time before morning. I began to believe they wet their beds to get even with me, and I said unkind things in frustration. As soon as the words spilled from my lips, I regretted my outburst of anger and hated myself afterward.

We attended church twice on Sundays and prayer meeting on Wednesday nights. Sunday mornings were very hectic. Arising extra early, I prepared dinner, set the timer on the oven to turn on and off at a certain time so our meal would be ready when we returned home from church. Dressing me was near impossible; I was always running around at the last minute trying to get the children ready too. Frequently I had to redress one or both because they soiled their clothes. When we finally arrived at church, I was not in a very spiritual mood because of previous thoughts that went through my mind. Short tempered, I said things I was ashamed of later when I had time to think about what happened, usually during the sermon.

The daily routine of housework, laundry, planning meals and keeping the children busy occupied most of my waking hours. Instead of starting my day in God's word with personal devotions and prayer, I did not think to nurture my relationship with Jesus. I exhausted myself striving to be a good wife and mother instead. Striving to please, I was overly disappointed in myself for repeated failure to change negative reactions, conscious only to the building anxiety within my spirit, I had no clue another driving force predominated and motivated my subconscious mind.

Welcome New Experiences

Experiencing good health throughout pregnancy prepared me for thirty-three hours of difficult labor. God blessed us with a perfect beautiful baby boy we named Dana after going through a painful delivery. My mother-in-law was a tremendous help keeping the older children at bay so I could rest and cleaned the house on Saturday, as was her usual routine. I fretted when she ran the vacuum cleaner under Dana's crib while he slept, but benefited later, loud noises did not disturb his sleep at naptime.

His parents moved to Florida when I was strong enough to handle housekeeping and our three children on my own. I wrote a six-page letter to them faithfully every week for many years. I missed my father-in-law; we were so much alike, spontaneous and silly. He never commented but I knew from the look he gave that he empathized more to my favor when his son and I had a spat.

Settling in to our quaint suburban area, the people were friendly. A young couple with four young children lived across the street. They welcomed us to the neighborhood and became good friends. The young woman admirably, seemed to have a firm grip on life and their children. Observing her expertise as a homemaker, she proudly boasted her many talents baking bread, canning vegetables and made pies, cookies and other neat things from scratch. Desiring to learn, I asked if she would teach me. After getting our husbands off to work, she came over and I began a course in home economics. I learned easy receipts to make bread and rolls then taught my children. They were excited to make their own special loaf and I loved to watch them mimic me as we went through the motions of kneading, rolling and punching down the risen mass of dough.

I became a skilled homemaker achieving tasks that I said earlier in our relationship I would never attempt. Proud of my accomplishments my husband, as was his usual custom, complimented me after each meal with a little more enthusiasm. I baked several loaves of bread every other day enjoying the "ooohs" and "ahhhs" when the freshly baked loaves came out of the oven. My family fell over each other wanting to get the first hot slice.

I learned many new skills from my neighbor and was soon designing and creating decorations for our home. Sewing and crafts became my channel to escape inner conflicts I wrestled with in my mind. Beaming with a sense of pride and accomplishment, each finished item I proudly displayed when my husband came home from work. He commented some things were nice and others I wasted my time on, dampening my enthusiasm. Not realizing he had a right to express his opinion, I did not receive his comment objectively, interpreting his entire reply negatively. I shied away from certain kinds of confrontation; to clarify a situation was not a comfortable conversational debate I desired to engage in. I wished I could, but insecurity controlled my thoughts and I feared that if I said something he did not like, he would love me less.

Each evening after our evening meal, we prayed together and read the Bible, memorized Bible verses and had fun competing as we learned and recited scripture aloud. Memorization came easy to the children and me.

Caring for a newborn was a new experience; I had no idea how to remedy problems such as severe colds and constipation, and called upon my neighbor for help. Initially, I enjoyed breast feeding but after five months getting up every two hours, I was so washed out and exhausted, my husband intervened, and one morning in the wee hours when the baby started crying, he got up and closed the door to the baby's room, then ours. He told me to stay put and get some rest. I laid there listening as the baby's cry grew more demanding and couldn't get back to sleep thinking I better not disobey my husband or he would stop loving me.

It did not take long for resentment to slither in and join the other subconscious insecurities, having to take time away from my newborn to meet the needs of the older children. Remembering a statement I made while dating, I commented that I loved his children as though they were mine. He responded I could never love his the way I would love my own flesh and blood because his children were not flesh of my flesh, again hurting my feelings at the time, but after I gave birth to my son I remembered his words. In hindsight, I knew they were true. I tried not to show favoritism; continuously analyzing the amount of time spent with my son and the time I devoted to his children, always feeling guilty. Mental and emotional exhaustion consumed my energy ninety percent of each day.

I had far too many unresolved issues plaguing my thoughts and the older children got the short side of my patience. To my point of view, being a step mom was more work than pleasure, especially to children that needed so much more than I could give them.

One of God's Lesson Plans -
Learning to Trust Him

On sunny days, I intermittently engaged in the children's play and nightly, my husband and I read Bible stories to them at bedtime. Before snuggling into bed, we knelt and prayed for each other, their grammas', grandpas', the missionaries in foreign countries, and people we knew needing prayer. When God answered, we celebrated and thanked Jesus.

The winter months were descending and I began silently praying for warmer clothing for our older children and more specifically for long sleeved undershirts for Dana, only God and I knew my request. Our pastor's wife put aside some outfits her children had outgrown. Thinking she would offend the receiver, she hesitated then added a few other items on top of the stack of garments before packing them in a box, obedient to the prodding of the Holy Spirit. She phoned and asked if we were in need of winter clothing to which I responded affirmatively. Later that day she delivered the package; I thanked her. The children were anxious to try on their new attire and gathered around as I opened the care package. Surprised, humbled, and very grateful to my Heavenly Father, tears spontaneously began streaming down my cheeks as I knelt starring at three perfect little long sleeved undershirts. They asked why I was crying. I shared my prayer request and the fact that only God and I knew what I prayed for, then held up the heaven sent gifts and explained that God really does hear us when we pray in secret. We thanked Jesus for answering my prayer and the warm winter clothing for them. God has extraordinary ways to reassure us of His presence, this significant example I would remember for the rest of my life!

Later when I had a chance to thank my pastor's wife, she confided that initially she had a dilemma deciding whether to include her infant's undergarments, concerned the recipient might be offended to receive second-hand underwear. "God impressed my heart to include them," she explained. Once I shared my prayer with her, we saw God's divine intervention turn her quandary into two personalized blessings, convinced we are not ultimately in control, He is. Praise God.

Ten months following the delivery of my son, I conceived again. Initially disappointed, I knew I was not physically or emotionally ready for another baby. In my third month of pregnancy while doing laundry in the basement, I became dizzy and fainted. My husband rushed to my aid and noticed I was hemorrhaging. He called our town's Emergency Medical Service and with sirens blaring, they rushed me to the hospital. Recalling my initial disappointment I deeply feared, God *is* going to take my child *because of the thoughts I entertained when I found out I was pregnant again.* Guilt laden and panic stricken my worse nightmare would come true, I pled with God not to take my baby.

*"Why in the world would I think God would take my children if I said or thought anything negative?" For years, I could not comprehend why I felt so profoundly convicted to believe such a frightful thought. The Holy Spirit revealed **that particular fear** resulted from a painful childhood experience impregnated deep within my subconscious memory now freshly exposed; my mom conceived while going through menopause. She explained I was going to have a little brother or sister and I was elated. I accidentally overheard her confess disappointment to be with child so late in life, then, later that day I observed her whisked away in an ambulance. Being too young to fully understand, I recalled the heart wrenching, utter despair not knowing whether she would live or die, venting to a grownup my wish to die if she didn't come home. Two weeks later, she did come home very depressed (to have miscarried); upon my inquiry, she sadly explained God took my little brother to heaven. The revealed memory exposed, I released the erroneous fear.*

My doctor stayed close by and shared humorous incidents about urine specimens and delivering babies. We laughed the time away, no further bleeding occurred after a few hours. He suggested I go home and take it easy doing housework. I laughed at the "take it easy" advice. How could I when three children needed constant attention and a demanding housework schedule filled every waking hour? However, I did heed his wise counsel and six months later gave birth to a beautiful red haired baby girl, red heads being predominant to his side of the family. We named our precious child. I offered several thankful heart filled prayers to God for not taking her in my earlier months of pregnancy.

Our baby cried so much from colic that she frazzled everyone's nerves. Six weeks into her young life while bathing her one morning, I noticed two little lumps on each side of her public bone, I thought the reason she fussed so much. The pediatrician explained surgery would correct the problem, but she was a bit underweight. The doctor assured waiting a few more months would not endanger her life.

My mom visited often. Dana squealed "mageek" when he saw his grandmother's car pull into our driveway and eagerly met her at the front door. She adored all four of our children. Listening to my woe filled complaints about the older children, her advice was to just give them love; eventually they will respond. I felt better after her visits.

A few years slipped quickly by since her cancer surgery. I began to notice her pace a little slower, her left arm never returned to its normal size, and her voice sounded raspy. She did not let on that she was feeling tired and weak more often but I knew something was wrong and worried about her. When her visits tapered off I phoned a couple of times a day. On nice days, I bundled the children up warmly and walked to her house. Rainy days I begged a ride from someone at church.

My mom's condition continued to worsen. My dad had developed adult type diabetes and needed care too. A few months later, she requested my older brother and his wife move in with them.

We celebrated Thanksgiving with turkey and all the trimmings. Her cancer spread rapidly, and by late December, she became bedridden. I felt so helpless, my mother's life was ebbing away right before my eyes; I felt like I was dying inside too. I wanted to stay but I had responsibilities of a family and felt so torn to leave after each visit.

Our baby was six months old when she went through surgery. As soon as she was well enough to travel, we visited grandma. My older children loved my mom and were upset to see her so sick. They scrambled onto her bed; Dana snuggled beside her. Placing our infant in her arms, her eyes filled with tears as she unwrapped the blanket to inspect her granddaughter's operation. Seeing the stitches still intact, she remarked her granddaughter looked like a tiny stuffed turkey; tearfully we all chuckled.

My brother and sister in law's faith dictated our religious holidays as non-celebratory to them so she did not set up our traditional tree at Christmas for my mom. Finding the small silver tree in the basement, I set it in her room and tearfully decorated it knowing this would be her

127

last Christmas with us. We talked about her relationship with Jesus. She told me she had invited Him in her heart when she was a young girl in her early teens, but knew she had not lived her life pleasing to God. I reminded her of the great men and women in the Bible who did not please God all the time; they sinned too. I read Romans 3:21 to 26 But now a righteousness from God, apart from law, has been made known, to which the Law and the Prophets testify. This righteousness from God comes through faith in Jesus Christ to all who believe. There is no difference, for all have sinned and fall short of the glory of God, and are justified freely by his grace through the redemption that came by Christ Jesus. God presented Him as a sacrifice of atonement, through faith in His blood. He did this to demonstrate His justice, because in His forbearance He had left the sins committed beforehand unpunished-- He did it to demonstrate His justice at the present time, so as to be just and the one who justifies those who have faith in Jesus. I praised her for insisting I attend church. Reciting her exact words: "one hour is not going to kill you" even threatening if I did not go, I could not play with my friends for the rest of the day. Through her persistence, I have a personal faith in Jesus as my Savior too. I suggested she confess whatever things she did wrong that came to her mind keeping her separated from her Savior and ask His forgiveness for them. I recited 1 John 1: 8 and 9 from the Bible, 8If we claim to be without sin, we deceive ourselves and the truth is not in us. 9If we confess our sins, He is faithful and just and will forgive us our sins and purify us from all unrighteousness. Those are His promises and His reassurance He would forgive all her sin. I hugged her and cried as I laid my head on her breast knowing I had to leave soon, but could not tear myself away. Hearing a car horn in the driveway, I kissed her goodbye. Functioning day to day was anxiety filled not knowing when the dreaded phone call would come.

On January 4, 1972 my sister in law phoned and said to come quickly; mom's condition changed drastically, she felt her death was imminent. I phoned several people for a ride but no one was home. Worrying about time slipping by so quickly, I prayed asking God to help then called a woman I knew from church and caught her just as she was about to step out her door. I pled for a ride; she came immediately and on the way, we prayed I would arrive in time. As I entered my mother's room and gazed upon her frail silhouette lying in bed, her face looked peaceful, as though she accomplished the confession to Jesus that she began the last time I visited, and knew He was waiting for her.

Tears flooded my eyes. I reflected on the times I wished God would take her, yet torn because I really wanted her to stay too. Kneeling beside her bed, I quietly sobbed choking on my words, and told her I loved her and was going to miss her. She weakly whispered to love my children and my stepchildren as she so often advised. I hugged her for the last time, conveyed my love for her again, and within a few minutes, she was gone. I would not see her again this side of heaven but confident my sweet mother will greet me when I get there and we will have a wonderful reunion.

I needed my mom to help me through life's struggles and could not shake the feeling of being abandoned, orphaned when she died. How I wished we had more years together knowing what I know today. Remorsefully I reminisced the many times I was unkind to her.

As a geriatric nurse, I observe families as they interact with their elderly parents, and make it a point to compliment them for spending precious moments together. My heart aches when I hear people speak unkind words to their aging parents. Being unkind leads to regret and remorse later in life, what is said cannot be taken back or erased. God blesses us with one set of parents and commands us to honor them, so that our days may be long. God knows what is best, and if He tells us to do something, we benefit from His wise advice if we obey Him. The experience we gain from the consequence of our actions shapes us into the people God plans us to become, tender not only towards our parents but also tender towards all of mankind.

After my mom's funeral, I busied myself raising my children but emotionally I felt like a lost child who needed mothering. I missed my mother desperately. I could no longer pick up the phone and call her nor could I make up for the many times I was unkind. I buried those thoughts and numbly carried on with life.

Eventually, our baby grew out of the crying, colicky stage and settled down to a routine that we could all live with. She was independent right from the start and such a delight to watch as she learned to overcome obstacles that blocked her way. Each one of our four children invited Jesus into their heart when they were young. We were a happy family as long as we stayed very busy. Being home with my children, I relived some of the fun I had in my childhood by interacting with them in their play each day. I knew how to have fun. Hot summer days we went swimming at a nearby lake to cool off when the weather turned unbearable. The children were very inventive and filled the wheelbarrow with water on days we were unable to get to the lake. They splashed and played to their hearts content in their pretend pool.

Fall was my favorite time of year. I loved the coolness of the season walking through the fallen leaves, observing the contrast of crisp colors on trees against the clear blue sky with its white puffy clouds scattered throughout. One warm day the children and I worked outside clearing the yard of dead branches that fell from the trees during a windy rainstorm a few days previous. I raked the leaves into huge piles and noted the children huddled together pointing in my direction, then each stole an armful from the heap I painstakingly gathered together and giggled as they passed back and forth, depositing their load against the house underneath the window. We stopped to refuel on hot chocolate and cookies. I busied myself in the kitchen, the children ran off to play outside. Each came bounding in the back door several times but never saw any child exit. Suspicious of their antics I followed their laughter to the back bedroom and glanced in the doorway viewing the window wide open with one child standing on the ledge posed to soar. Before I could utter a word, he leaped out. I ran to the window expecting an injury to the fearless jumper. Instead, I saw them having the time of their lives rolling in and throwing leaves, laughing at each other.

When winter rolled around, a nearby park with a pond provided a great place to ice skate; when school was cancelled the six of us bundled up warmly and headed off to our favorite golf course to go sledding, always ending the day with our traditional snack of hot chocolate and cookies when we returned home. Other snow days, their dad heaped a gigantic pile of snow off to the side of the driveway and helped them build a snow fort after he finished shoveling. The children and I created ornaments for our Christmas tree from scraps of material, loose feathers from pillows, glitter, empty egg cartons, and whatever else we could find. We had a fun time together making our very own treasurers.

My husband handled the finances and budgeted just so much for food each week, so I learned to be very creative with meal preparation. We lived meagerly while he attended school. The children wore hand me down clothing donated from our neighbor across the street and people we knew at church. Cash was scarce; we were always pinching pennies every holiday. I felt guilty unable to provide little extras for our children. One spring in particular unexpected expenses ate into our food budget. My husband and I prayed for a miracle but planned on a simple meal for our Easter dinner. Prompted by the Holy Spirit, a generous family from church provided a completely cooked ham dinner and while we were at church, delivered the care package to our back door. Arriving home and discovering the food, still warm, we thanked God and asked Him to bless whoever provided our delicious Easter dinner. As each person's birthday arrived, I prepared his or her favorite meal for supper, and for dessert, we celebrated with a happy birthday ice cream cake.

My husband worked diligently through school and graduated from college in three years with a Bachelor of Arts degree. A teaching contract from a very prestigious town about twenty miles south of our home; afforded him a significantly higher salary than the surrounding towns in our area presented new graduates.

We enrolled our oldest daughter in kindergarten when she turned five. Her first day of school, I helped her up the steps into the school bus, then turned and cried as I walked back to the house. One by one, my playmates dwindled. With the last child off to school, I fulfilled the promise I made to my mom and obtained my high school equivalency.

Before our son was born, I rearranged the living room and bedroom furniture weekly; my mom used to do the same, as she cleaned she rearranged the furniture. I tried my hand at carpentry one day while my husband was at school and redesigned our tiny clothes closet into a shallow walk in by altering the poles to fit widthwise, one side for his clothes and one for mine. He was surprised but did not make a fuss. I had been nursing our newborn for two months routinely waking to his crying at two in the morning. One night I wearily arose, groped my way in the dark to the door to our room, opened it and walked through backward hoping not to awake my husband then turned and pulled the door closed releasing the doorknob. After I took a step, I realized I had walked into our clothes closet. Unable to locate the doorknob in that tiny pitch-black space, I called for help then paused hearing my husband's laughter on the other side of the door. He opened the door and chuckled again as I stood there with his dress shirt wrapped partially around my face. I stopped rearranging things for a while.

An amusing incident recalled from childhood popped into my thoughts as I reminisced my closet escapade. My dad came home from work late one night and retired to their darkened bedroom, which was directly down the hall from mine. A few moments later, I heard his clothes drop to the floor followed by a loud thud; then his question, "Rose did you move the bed again?" I giggled to myself. Remembering that incident still amuses me.

One evening sitting on the couch together, he talked about knocking out the wall separating the kitchen and living room. The mission sounded exciting, I nodded affirmatively. He jumped up and retrieved "big Bertha," his heavy-duty wrecking bar from his truck, then smashed a big hole in the middle of the wall. We stayed up into the wee hours of the early morning demolishing and cleaning up the debris altering the living room into a dining room overnight. The young couple across the street had a four-foot round wagon wheel they lugged home from their trip to Maine and showed it to my husband. I guessed the men made a deal because we wound up with it. Creative at making unusual things, my hubby fashioned a unique one of kind dining room table from the wagon wheel. He special ordered a round piece of Plexiglas with a hole cut from the center to accommodate the hub of the wheel and constructed a sturdy cradle for the base. The children used the tabletop like an enormous large lazy- susan and spun it around to deliver items someone requested from the other side of the table. Often I did not know if the plate in front of me was mine when I returned to the table after retrieving something in the kitchen.

We began to feel cramped not having a living room, so my husband undertook odd jobs after school. He planned to add a sixteen by thirty two foot addition to the back of our home and answered an ad in the paper to dismantle an old barn in the country. Discovering the wood used to construct the barn to be from the Chestnut tree; it had the unique qualities he was looking for to remodel our home and asked permission to keep the material he dismantled. Imagining what he planned to do, he shared his thoughts with me. I could not mentally envision anything unless I saw a picture. I presumed he was often frustrated because I could not enter into that artistic world with him.

He paneled the foyer and our new dining room with the chestnut wood and replaced the picture window with a six-foot bow window then installed another six-foot bow in our bedroom to present a symmetrical look to the outside of our home The installation of wide plank flooring finished off the dining room. My husband admired the unique look of the foyer and our dining room and began searching for more chestnut wood to remodel the rest of the house.

The children and I demolished the back porch and steps while my husband taught school during the day. After the cement for the foundation hardened, we had a huge patio to enjoy for the summer months. We acquired lawn furniture and spent time outdoors while my husband worked to replenish extra cash to buy lumber for the addition. We had a few picnics and stayed up late enjoying our outdoor retreat as we watched the children catch fireflies at night; and listened to tree toads chirp away to one another. We began to argue about money spent for what I though were foolish expenditures. I did not communicate our needs. I thought he would just know. I suppose he tuned out my complaining day after day.

Learning Diversified Skills

We all helped frame out the new living room addition the following year. We worked together to sheet rock the walls and ceiling. I enjoyed working alongside my hubby and learned valuable skills measuring, and using power tools.

Our friends and neighbor helped install a ten-foot bow window. I made curtains to match the style in our dining room. Plans for a garage were next. We discussed where the door should go to the entrance. I disagreed with his suggestion. He built it where he chose, and had to squeeze his way around our full-size truck to get from the garage to the house. I jested he should have listened to me; he did not like my teasing.

The Highway Department was in the process of clearing properties to accommodate a connector ramp to the thruway, and a few houses were marked for demolition. On our way home from church one Sunday my husband spotted a large white ten room house that was designated to be removed, and stopped to take a closer look at it. The foundation structure was comprised of unblemished chestnut beams, the fireplace, constructed of handmade bricks. Excitedly he commented he wished there were some way we could obtain some of the beams for our home.

After noting the name of the company on the sign, I prayed then called the general contractor and made an appointment to see him the following day while my husband was at work. I do not remember what I said or how I phrased my request but I convinced him to let us dismantle the house for the wood and contents. Only God could have influenced his heart that day because his answer stunned me. He drew up a contract releasing him of any responsibility of injury to any of our family members while on the property and I signed my name on the dotted line. He told me to notify him when we retrieved what we wanted, he would clean up after we were through. I was doubly shocked at his statement to clean up.

I thought I would have to pick my husband up off the floor when I told him where I went, who I saw, and what I did, then presented the contract I signed. We wasted no time and loaded ladders, his wrecking bar and a whole mess of tools in the back of our station wagon, piled into the car and drove to the house. My husband set up the ladder alongside the house, grabbed big Bertha, and climbed to the roof to inspect it more closely. He started removing shingles, carefully pulling the nails to free a board. He exclaimed the roof's construction consisted of unusually wide chestnut boards. It took a week to remove the roof and the top of the chimney, careful to not break his rare find. The entire house structure built of beautiful 8X8 chestnut beams were mortise and tendon jointed, coupled together with fat pegs where the mortise met the tendon. He rigged a pulley mechanism being cautious for his safety, carefully knocked out the wooden pegs one at a time, then carefully attached each freed beam to the pulley and cautiously lowered it to the ground. He was quite amazing to watch as he figured out which beam to remove first and next. If he removed the wrong one, all could crash to the ground and kill him in the process. Using the pulley mechanism, each of us; our older son was ten, our older daughter, eleven; my husband and I loaded one beam at a time on top of our station wagon and after securing it to the car, transported it to our house two miles away. One of the beams was so heavy it dented the roof rack of our station wagon. As we disassembled the central fireplace, our youngest children carried the bricks one or two at a time and loaded them in the back of the station wagon. An elderly man driving an old, beat up pick up truck stopped and asked for the copper pipes from the plumbing fixtures and any metal fixtures we didn't want. We gave him most every metal thing there was in the house; he drove away a very happy man.

Another fellow came by and asked if we needed help. We thanked him but declined his offer. He asked if we had come across any wood flooring we did not want. My husband told him he was about to pull up the linoleum covering one of the bedroom floors. The person stated he would be back in the morning, and drove off. Pulling up the brittle pieces of linoleum, we found an oak floor. It looked almost brand new. My husband thought prying it up would require bruit strength but the nails that held the boards were so worn they literally burst out with a dirt shovel. Actually, the first plank he pried with the shovel flew up and

135

landed a couple of feet from where I stood watching him work. It took all of twenty minutes to remove the entire floor. I stacked the boards neatly in what was left of the living room.

The fellow arrived early the next morning. Finding the boards in such pristine condition, he enthusiastically thanked us, loaded them on his vehicle and drove away a very happy man.

An unusual telltale sign the house was built in the 1800's, we discovered a silver Indian head nickel dated in the 1800's lying underneath one of the stair treads about half way up the staircase, of the main stairwell. Researching histories of homes, it was a custom to mark the date the house was built in that fashion. Disassembling the chimney, we found dozens of empty liquor bottles hidden behind the walls in the attic, old boxes of letters meticulously tied with ribbon and newspapers haphazardly stacked in small piles.

I realized later, I uncaringly threw away interesting family history of the people who lived there. The world I was concerned with was my husband and children. God continued working His plan to broaden my perspective and horizon of the world around me. I needed to see people and the world through the eyes of Jesus.

Reminiscing the enormous task of dismantling a ten room house and finishing in twenty seven days with only minor injuries led me to truly believe God had appointed angels to assist our efforts and protect us; giving extraordinary strength to physically accomplish feats humanly impossible for our little family members to do.

A Difficult Time Ahead

My dad remained in his home for two years with my older brother and sister in law after my mom died. His disposition grew more ornery towards my brother and his wife as his health declined. He sold his home, moved in with us, and appointed my husband Power of Attorney to his checking account to pay his expenses. From the very first day he was non compliant to his diabetic diet and often ate the snacks I prepared for the children.

We began the house-wrecking project early in May and labored industriously morning to dark. Three weeks into our project, my father expired. We ceased our contracted work for three days. Quite insistently, my dad stipulated months ago we keep the remainder of his estate, as opposed to sharing equally with my brothers; again, he chose my husband to oversee his request. My husband left the final choice to me after my dad died. Selfishly I chose to keep it reasoning it would be wonderful to pay the college loan that strangled our finances and buy the kids new clothes and shoes for a change instead of wearing hand me downs from others. After settling my father's bills we paid off the government loan, purchased new clothes and shoes for the kids and then bought an old used camper so we could spend time together camping.

Resuming the demolition project, we salvaged several thousand bricks from the central fireplace and stacked them along the driveway. I chipped mortar from the ends and side one brick at a time. My husband built a sixteen-foot long trough in our back yard and lined it with Polyethylene to soak the beams in a special chemical before he could utilize them for the living room addition. The walls and ceiling he decided to paint flat black to camouflage the vacant knotholes that were observable in the chestnut planks planned for paneling. At the paint store, he ordered several cans of flat black. The clerk asked what we intended to do with so many gallons of black paint. "Paint our new living room addition," we replied. I would not venture to guess what he thought as he walked away shaking his head.

The first few months slipped by quickly as we worked cleaning the beams and wood. I scraped all the bug bodies and soot that covered the top layer, then removed the broken and rusted nails. To bring out the beauty of the wood it needed scraping with a hand plane. The whole process took nearly the whole day. Lastly, I waxed each board, stopping in between each phase to do my usual household chores. I learned short cuts and became more efficient, managing to complete three boards per day. My job was difficult and messy. Splinters difficult to remove began discouraging my efforts. My husband complimented me when he came home from work each day. It took him all of a half hour at the most to nail the boards in place on the wall. It took the whole day to prepare that wood and only ten minutes to hang it. Each day I faced another pile of dirty boards. My attitude soured somewhere in the process, I became irritable and impatient having to live in dirt and soot, and I resented having to do all the dirty work, not to mention the splinters. My hands were sore and I hated the mess from the wood shavings. Musty smelling dust from planning the boards all day clogged my nose making breathing uncomfortable. I pretended to enjoy the work. There were times when I wanted to scream, why should I do the dirty work? I could not express my increasing irritation, because conflicting messages fed apprehension to my conscience, I did not want to disappoint my husband; he would stop loving me.

We were able to panel the entire room with the wide chestnut planks, including the ceiling. It was nearly impossible to detect the nail and knotholes. The chestnut rafters he cut to the width of our ceiling; notched out new mortise and tendon joints and strategically positioned and locked them in place across and at each end of the living room ceiling tying all the beams together with pegs whittled from the short leftover ends. To the far outside corner of the room, my husband set an eight-foot wide semi circular floor and put up a four-foot high half wall with a portion of the bricks confiscated from the central fireplace of the old house. A wood burning stove occupied the bricked area. Wall to wall carpeting finished the room. He searched for a fireplace design for our dining room that included a three-foot wide fire box opening, bread oven, and pass through wood box. We incorporated a barbecue pit above the small pass through opening and hired a mason to construct the

Eighteenth Century style fireplace. My husband added chestnut wood shelves above the large wood storage bins on either side of the fireplace, and paneled the tiny bit of wall with left over chestnut wood surrounding the bow window in the dining room. We had a few large beams left over so he added them to the ceiling and walls strategically placing them so they looked like they had always been a structural part of the house. The dining room was completed. Remodeling consumed several years but when finished, it was beautiful and cozy.

One rainy evening, a woman, a complete stranger knocked at our front door. She explained that she drove by our house to and from work observing our progress each day remodeling. She remarked it looked so interesting from the street her curiosity got the best of her and she just had to see our home from the inside. We welcomed and showed her around; explaining how we obtained all our material from an old house, we disassembled here in town. I gave a brief dissertation of cleaning and preparing the wood before we could use it for our intended purpose. Quite impressed, she thanked us for sharing.

The last project we added was a ten by ten greenhouse to the back of our addition, an attractive touch to our Early American style home. Organic gardening then became our interest. We subscribed to an organic gardening magazine and read every piece of literature pertaining to growing organic vegetables. We learned how to companion plant, make natural organic formulas for feeding the vegetation, and insect repellent from the juice of hot red pepper plants to keep the bugs away.

He tilled most of our property in the front, side and back of our yard, ordered organic soil, which we found out later was mixed with cow manure from a farm in the country, and added the necessary nutrients to establish our garden.

Freckles our dog, part hunter; part collie had long brown and white fur. I did not know why she insisted on rolling in dirt after giving her a bath, but found out canine Hunters camouflage their scent that way. She disappeared for a short time after the delivery of soil , then reappeared covered with dirt and manure. She smelled awful. Removing all the manure from her fur took a very long time. When she was a pup, I shrieked and chased after her for mishaps in the house, frightening as I attempted to swat her with the broom, frustrated at having to clean up her mess as well as everyone else's. Impatient attempting to housebreak her, I had enough work to do, She bared her teeth only once, I thought she smiled; at least it looked that way to me. I immediately changed my tone of voice and patted her head. She smiled again, I suppose in anxiousness not knowing what I was going to do next. Each time I raised my voice she smiled. Eventually, she smiled on command.

The greenhouse off our new addition provided sunshine and warmth, as early as January. I began sowing various vegetable seeds and nurtured the seedlings until the weather turned warm enough to transplant them in the garden. We planted everywhere the sun shone brightly on our little piece of property. Everyone had a job to do. Our garden was fun at first caring for the vegetables, but as the growing season dragged on gardening became a chore. The children complained about having to pull weeds, and I complained about having too many vegetables to clean and store. Sometimes I stayed up until early morning hours to preserve or freeze the vegetables. We had a rich wonderful garden for several years, and even though I complained, I felt a sense of pride and accomplishment serving the produce of our labor each evening at supper.

The children and I went apple picking and berry hunting in the fall after my neighbor taught me how to make jelly. The jelly that didn't gel we used as a topping on pancakes; one of the kids experimented and mixed the liquid in their milk making blueberry, raspberry, strawberry or apple milk shake. Nothing went to waste.

One year around Thanksgiving holiday, my hubby brought home a humongous pumpkin. It must have been about three or four feet around, (well it seemed that big anyway) and was a challenge to clean and cook but it yielded over seventeen pumpkin pies.

Teaching was my husband's passion, he had acquired a reputation for bringing out the best in each child he taught by making learning fun for his students; and received many complimentary notes from parents. Pleasured by the attention received he was often invited to dine with the parents of his students. On occasion, he phoned to say he would be late; I would have to lead our devotional time after supper. His call upset me and I could not read the Bible or pray with our children. Feeling stressed, I thought he preferred not to come home to me. When his phone calls dictated for me not to wait up for him, I became intensely jealous of the people he spent time with as his popularity increased. Insecurity and fear controlled negative thoughts, and my imagination ran wild. Why is he late I asked myself, maybe he is seeing someone else. Thoughts played repeatedly in my mind until I saw his car pull into the driveway. When he asked about devotions, my mind went blank; I could not answer him at first then managed to say we did not have devotions. He looked disappointed and asked for an explanation. My mind went blank again and all I could offer was a feeble excuse. I did not know what stopped me from communicating my real feelings and the fears I had at the time.

My husband and I attended a few social events in the town where he taught school. When introduced to a group of people, a poor self-image worked against me and I felt stupid having nothing to contribute to conversations and could not identify with affluent intellectual people. He, on the other hand, had no trouble socializing and often walked away with someone during a conversation. As each person strolled off, I found a quiet room and waited for him. At one occasion, a pretty, well-dressed woman asked my husband to join her and her husband for dinner. Assuming I was included too, I responded we would love to. She stated rather curtly, "Oh, no dear, I didn't mean you too." I felt humiliated. I was jealous and did not want to share my husband with those beautiful intelligent women. I imagined the situation to be a set up for infidelity, and could not believe he would even think of attending any dinner party without me. We discussed the invitation all the way home, and at home also. He accused me of imagining things that were not true, the woman was happily married and there was nothing to fear. I remembered a story he related about his coworker cheating on his wife with one of those "happily married" lonely women that's business trips took their husband away for weeks at a time. My sense of "woman's intuition" dictated to stand firm, responding I was not stupid and dictated he decline the invitation if I could not attend.

*The underlying emotional feeling of abandonment I experienced as a child began to affect my emotions and the same uneasiness overshadowed them. I was not aware of the **why** feeling abandoned just the deep feeling of emptiness in my spirit. I became very possessive of his attention afraid to loose him to someone else.*

Our oldest son was incorrigible, defiant to us and at school. Researching various options, we decided to register him in an educational program located in the Dominican Republic recognized to rehabilitate delinquent adolescents. For parents, system policy dictated no visits for the first three months so they could acclimate the children to rules and regulations.

My husband planned a mini vacation for us for a few days at an exclusive resort a few miles from where his son attended school. After we visited, we headed to the resort for a little rest and relaxation before going home to the realities that awaited us. We were told that busses ran to and from the resort daily...hourly in fact. We waited three hours in the scorching heat along the highway. Busses whizzed by. My husband flagged down a dilapidated taxi that looked like it came straight from a junkyard. The car stopped and one of the two men got out, took our bags and put them in the trunk, opened the back door and we got in. The driver asked our destination, my husband responded. They started speaking Spanish to each other as we drove off. My husband understood every word. The man driving announced the car needed gas, turned off the main road and drove down a one-lane dirt road, turning several times before we came to a stop in a secluded area along side a tiny shack that had a gas pump next to it. The driver got out and filled the tank. The other man got out and joined the driver. My husband got out and stretched his arms and legs, listening to their conversation as the men walked a short distance away. I sat in the car and waited. A woman dressed in tattered clothing approached my window and begged for money. Her breath reeked of alcohol. My husband quietly told her in Spanish to go away and she disappeared into a tall-weeded area. The men approached my husband and they talked. He stepped back in the car with me, the driver got in leaving the other man behind, and we departed for the resort. Once inside the security gate, we got out and our driver retrieved the luggage from the trunk. My husband spoke quietly to the security guard, then turned to speak to the driver. All previous conversations with him were in English, and the man looked astounded when my husband said something in Spanish to him. The guard then spoke up and ordered him to leave and never come back. One evening as the two of us were relaxing watching TV my husband told me the story that actually took place in the secluded area. What I perceived to be a conflict between the men was actually an argument between them. They planned to kill us for our belongings and money. My husband did some fast talking and explained we did not have anything of value but if one of them would drive us to our resort he promised to get enough money so he and his friend would never have to work again. Once safely inside the resort, he told the driver that he was not going to give him any money; not being turned in to the police was payment enough. He admitted to being scared to death for our lives and prayed earnestly for God's protection.

We returned to the US two weeks later and fell back into normal routines of daily living at home. Bed-wetting and constant bickering agitated and stressed me out ninety percent of the day. I tried to be more patient, but I could not control my frustration and growing anger, guilt occupied my thoughts. I began my usual complaining. Striving through the next few years to be a little more patient and a better mother, only heaped more stress to my over burdened emotions. Old feelings and fears still skillfully hidden in my subconscious, played more intensely with my thoughts. Be deficient in communication to express true feelings led me to react to his lack of understanding with fits of impatience and intolerance. He asked my opinion before making decisions when we first got married. As the years progressed, he did not ask anymore. We had many disagreements and in frustration, when neither conceded one would end our stand off with "well you just want your way that's all, it has to be only your way." Communicating anything was frustrating. Important issues went unresolved. Intimidated, bound by thoughts that dictated insecurity motivated reactions I could not control. What ever I said sounded like a defensive attack at him for problems only I could solve, if I only knew what they really were. Many times after a heated verbal exchange, I felt frustrated because I did not know why I lost control of myself so easily.

Our prayer time together at night sounded like a teaching lesson instead of an intimate time of prayer with God. I thought he tried to lecture me through little things he said in prayer and did not want to pray with him any longer. He always began with Our Lord's Prayer, I quickly tired of the formality and made excuses not to pray with him, ignoring that still small voice prodding me to continue despite my feelings.

Little did I know it at the time but our son was duped into believing his chosen lifestyle was an acceptable way to live. I sensed something askew then but could not identify what. Hurt and angered when told what he embraced, not at him, but at Satan, life and myself. I was disappointed in myself because I failed to be a positive role model in marriage. If he lived in a more stable home, with a mom and dad who were devoted to each other he would not have preferred to embrace the lifestyle he choose; angered at life because that kind of lifestyle exists, and irate at Satan because he snared my boy and fed him lies. God is the only one that can fill the empty love spot in his life.

I pray for my son daily and I believe that someday he will see his choice only leads to unhappiness. I witnessed his prayer asking Jesus into his heart as a little boy and I truly believe God will enable my son to turn away from that lifestyle and return to a spirit filled life with his savior Jesus.

Our oldest daughter had gotten pregnant when she was sixteen years old. I could not face God and the people in church because I felt responsible for her getting pregnant. I made an appointment to see my pastor; he asked why I thought I felt responsible for the choice she made. Hearing truth that the decision to have sex and get pregnant was her choice not mine, enabled me to release the false guilt I carried. He prayed with me for God to give wisdom to overcome obstacles as they arose and I thanked him for helping me through the crisis.

A failed business venture forced us to sell our little home in the suburbs we spent so much time to remodel, to pay off the loans borrowed for expensive equipment purchased.

After we moved, our marriage continued on a slow downward spiral. Our oldest son was in his late teens and the home we purchased had a finished basement, which he claimed for his bedroom. One day while cleaning, I found a rather strange looking bottle in his closet and showed it to my husband. It turned out to be a bottle used to smoke hash. He confronted his son and told him he had to leave if he continued to use drugs.

My husband became friends with several couples from different countries and for some reason embraced their food preferences and our supper menu often varied at mealtime. Reminiscing, I surmise he truly desired to invite his friends to our home, but was too embarrassed because we lived so simply; next option was to broaden our taste buds by exposing us to various ethnic foods. He came home with new receipts and prepared them himself. Some we liked, others we would not touch; octopus with spaghetti especially.

His lasting friendship was with a Japanese couple that lived in the town where he taught school. The husband received notice to return to Japan in the middle of the school year; their daughter wished to finish her last year of high school in America. My husband opened our home, and her father consented to her living with us.

Our daughter shared her bedroom, and at first, they got along great. As the girl's social life increased, she had more activities to attend, my hubby drove her to wherever she needed to be. It appeared to the rest of us that he fussed over her and even changed our diet to make her feel more at home. Eating with chopsticks was difficult at first, but we acquired the knack and turned out to be a fun thing to do. As months passed, the children thought their father went overboard catering to our guest, and confided their jealousy to me. They were afraid to confront him because they did not know how he would react. I was jealous too, and envied the attention he gave her. My ridiculous fears and the mental tapes that played in my head were relentless, suggesting imaginary things they might be involved with together. Each in our own way tried to steal his attention from her. Her father dominated authority in her home. I supposed my husband desired to display his authority over us and ordered a ridiculous request to our son that did not make sense to him or me. At times I stood in defense of our children when I thought he was unfair but I decided to support my husband and stated he should obey his father; creating confusion in our son. He looked at me as if to say what is the matter with you mom; do you not see he is showing off his authority? He became hostile and verbally abusive toward both of us. Emotionally, I could not take any more and exploded, stating his unfairness and my jealousy at his favoritism showered on our houseguest. I wanted to physically beat on him but instead turned my anger toward my son and he and I wound up in a physical confrontation in the basement. When our eyes met, I saw confusion in his eyes. Suddenly he bolted out the door and down the driveway barefoot. In my frustration, I grabbed the first thing I saw and smashed his stereo equipment then in utter disgust at myself for loosing total control I threw myself down and cried, completely exhausted, drained, physically and emotionally, then dragged myself back upstairs. Returning to the kitchen, a police officer was standing, chatting with my husband; which totally mortified me. Enraged, I told the officer to leave he had no business in our home; we were capable of handling our own problems. I was furious with my husband for calling the police and thought he chose to further humiliate me.

After I calmed down, I hopped in my car and drove through the streets looking for my boy. When he spotted me, he ran the other way! I grieved at his response and sobbed. I hated my husband at that moment, and I hated myself. Remembering past moments when he was the aggressor in confrontations with his son I never thought to call the police; it would be thoughtless to disgrace and humiliate him. I did not like being angry and hostile. I hated violence and dropped out of life emotionally. I felt guilty, driving my son from our home. Our houseguest moved back to Japan and my husband was angered that I jeopardized his friendship with her father.

Life was a blur for the next few months, I could not resolve the dreadful altercation with my son; it played repeatedly in my thoughts. I worried about him constantly. My daughter could usually persuade me to come out of a slump but failed at everything she tried. She was fearful of her brother, and decided she did not want to live with us. My husband arranged for her to live with his sister in Florida. I pleaded with her not to leave. I mourned for my two children. Deep feelings of remorse plagued my heart.

Shortly after that incident, my husband said he wanted his freedom. He could not cope with the stress. I could not bear to be alone; I needed him for my existence and begged him to stay. We decided to seek marriage counseling, and went a few times to a wonderful pastor of a Baptist church in the next town. He counseled us together then separately, then gave us a written test. He offered suggestions to help rekindle love for each other. My thoughts dictated he was the one that needed to change, and he did try, but I excused his attempts, thinking his efforts were fake; he forced himself to be nice, it didn't come naturally, therefore attempts to jump-start our relationship were not successful. Stressful situations sliced off a piece of our marriage one bit at a time driving us farther apart.

I never allowed God time to heal my wounded spirit before we got married.

After what seemed like an eternity, my son returned home. My husband suggested I get a job to help pay bills. I decided to apply for a nurse's aide position, very different from the work experience I had. After completing the course, I received my certificate and worked part time as a Certified Nurses Aide. I liked the elderly, they were open honest and praised even the slightest kindness towards them.

God began working in my heart as I found nursing very rewarding internally in my emotions as well as externally interacting with precious needy people. Their praises caused me to realize I wasn't as mean as I thought. They complimented me in so many ways; I started to feel good inside when I was at work.

I finished up my assignments a few minutes early; as I waited to punch out I observed the medication nurse giving pills to each patient and decided I wanted to go to nursing school. My husband was elated when I told him and encouraged me. He and our son unselfishly took over cleaning and cooking so I could devote all my time to study.

Insecurities and anxieties started harassing me, instead of being appreciative, I felt threatened. I was not comfortable with anyone taking over my responsibilities as homemaker, mother and wife, the jobs I did for many years. Homemaker was my identity. I rejected their attempts to lighten my load as I studied. My insecurity drove me to test the depth of his love. I said and did things to drive him away from me still afraid to communicate my true feelings and fears. Neither had a clue to my emotional state.

Being out of school for so many years, I had difficulty studying. My husband found me asleep many times reading my textbooks. While I read, my mind wandered to thoughts of my daughter. I needed her home with me. I could not help thinking how much I missed her and wondered if she missed me. My husband suggested she address her mail to the school where he taught. I managed to sneak a couple of letters from his briefcase and read them disappointed she did not even ask about me. I did not receive a word from her for three years except for one Thanksgiving, my husband took time off from work and we flew down to see how she was doing. His sister picked us up from the airport. My daughter was waiting in the driveway. She gave her dad a hug, then me. Her hug felt like she had to force, I felt estranged. Knowing she did not want to come back with us made me feel miserable. I didn't know how to fix things between us.

I got angry when plans to go to church fell through, and blamed everyone for the poor choices I made while we were there. I was so distraught I didn't eat for three days.

We stayed about a week. On our way home, I came away believing she did not love me anymore because she did not want to return with us and convinced myself I would never see her again. Preoccupied with ways I could fix our broken relationship, when I went shopping, I found myself at the greeting card section starring at "miss you" cards for a long time. I thought about sending one, purchased it, and never mailed it.

Nursing school was stressful but one and a half years later, I passed my final exam. My son, husband and my pastor attended my graduation. I felt proud to become a nurse and proud that my son was there to see me graduate.

My first nursing situation was working with handicapped children. They were so needy; I grew to love each one of the nine young people I was responsible to. Each one had a unique personality and although they were physically handicapped, their spirit soared during every happy moment we spent together. They responded with giggles and high-pitched screams. I worked well with the other nurses and had a good reputation with the Director of Nurses. My first stressful incident involved two nurses' aides who did not like me and falsely accused me of acting inappropriately toward one of the residents; which prompted immediate dismissal. Wanting to prove my innocence, I had to take them to court; that entailed spending money I didn't have. The Director of Nursing confided her personal opinion and found me another job as a medication nurse at a nursing home. She wrote a letter to the D.O.N of that facility, gave a high recommendation, and they hired me. Through that incident, I grew stronger in my faith. I learned to trust God and worry less.

Even though our marriage was stressful, we stayed together. My job was secure, and I made a decent paycheck each week. My husband decided to sell our home when the real estate market was hot. He talked about purchasing a condominium to free up his time doing maintenance and yard work so we could spend more time together. We both loved camping, which influenced him to buy a conversion van so we could travel more. The van was mine to drive. We looked at a beautiful condominium in another town and I was encouraged thinking our marriage was going to change for the better. In midstream, he changed plans and instead, purchased an eight-room colonial that needed a lot of work. He planned to make a few minor changes, paint, and place it back on the market hoping to make a significant profit while the housing market presently boomed. As soon as our mortgage went through, the market went into a slump and we were stuck with the huge house. He suggested that I take over the payments and insurance premiums for the conversion van then suggested I obtain a credit card to establish my own credit line, in case anything ever happened to him. I had no clue of our financial state and questioned why I had to start paying bills. I was disappointed with the negative incidents that happened just when I had a glimmer of hope that we had a chance to spend more time together. I did an about face emotionally and became suspicious of his suggestion to establish myself apart from him in case "anything ever happened."

Three years passed since my daughter moved to Florida. We received a phone call; she wanted to come home. We picked her up from the airport and drove in silence on the way home. She was much more independent and I had difficulty at first trying to assimilate her independence and openness. We went shopping together frequently and she talked my ear off, one trait she never lost. I enjoyed her company; she kept my mind occupied with her chatter. I wore my feelings on my coat sleeve, so to speak; and she knew when something bothered me. I did not feel safe with anyone but her, I knew whatever I said she kept confidential. Often I felt like the child and she the adult and made dreadful choices telling her too much, confessing my unhappiness over the past several years, and how angry I was with her father for sending her away. She reacted by stating how disappointed she was to find nothing had changed between her father and I and advised me to divorce him. I thought about her suggestion. Discouraged, nothing *had* gotten any better, I searched the newspapers for places I could afford to rent: I found a condominium for sale and she and I went to check it out. Initially, I was excited about breaking up but after seriously thinking about my decision, I changed my mind. The next time she and I talked, I explained that her father and I were married in the presence of God and we made a covenant to Him and to each other, "for better or worse, in sickness and in health, until death do us part." I was in the marriage for better or worse. She was disappointed and asked me how much worse can it get being so unhappy all the time. Recalling how much I shared with her, I can see the heavy burdens I placed on her young shoulders. I should have had more confidence in my marriage partner and begin to try and share my feelings and fears with him.

Our daughter turned sixteen, took Drivers Ed in school and eventually earned her license. Her dad bought her a cute little gray car. She obtained a job part time working as a waitress in a pizza parlor after school, and made a lot of money. Being able to buy herself things we could not afford, she decided she wanted to quit school and work. I gave her the same advice my mom told to me, and as another incentive to stay in school we warned if she insisted on quitting, we would take her car away. She quit and my husband took the car. She angrily vented she no longer wanted to live with us and moved in with a girlfriend she worked with who lived about a half mile from our house.

Old fears surfaced, I blamed myself for our family not getting along and could no longer cope with the stress of her leaving again, and the emotional guilt I felt. I needed help and started seeing a Christian counselor. Each time I attended a counseling session I came away frustrated that I did not receive answers to my problems. I wanted instant results. When the counselor asked questions, I kept telling him that I felt responsible for everything.

The roots to my guilty conscience went much farther back in time than the incidents I could remember. No matter how hard I tried I could not get past recent memories.

I struggled searching for something deeper. I managed to recall a painful experience hurting my parents when I disobeyed them by marrying my first husband, an alcoholic. Both of my parents died years before I became aware of the anguish I put them through. I had no way to say I was sorry and sobbed thinking about the grief I caused them. I left that day feeling a little better about myself, especially after praying knowing I received forgiveness from God.

My next visit was more productive. I learned I was only responsible for things I did and said. When I **thought** people blamed me for poor decisions they made and things didn't work out the way they wanted, negative tapes began to play in my head...guilty, guilty. I immediately felt guilty again then remembered what my counselor told me. To counteract the emotional attack, I repeated out loud, "It's not my fault, it's your problem not mine." I said those words so often my husband asked, "whom are you trying to convince, you or me?" I got angry and wanted to express my true feelings, but I kept quiet. I thought if I did, he would walk out for good. I knew then, I still had not resolved inner conflicts that continued to torture my mind. Between car payments, insurance, and buying things from the shopping network, my paycheck was not large enough to continue counseling.

Wrong choice again, I should have stopped purchasing things from the shopping network so I could afford counseling. I had resolved a problem and made a positive step to combat the negative tapes that played in my head.

I came away from most sessions aggravated, so I stopped going. I loved spending money more on stuff that made me feel good. Our marriage was dying, more with each passing day. I could not communicate even though my husband encouraged me, and we drifted farther apart. My heart began to harden toward him. We were not attending church, not praying, and just existed from day to day. Throughout our marriage my husband repeatedly stated, "No matter what happens, I do not believe in divorce, divorce would never be an option," yet whenever we argued the first words out of his mouth were, "Maybe we should get divorced," making me feel insecure, worried he would walk out at any time.

The ultimate climax occurred one day shortly before Christmas. My husband informed me he could no longer live with my faults and wanted a divorce. For a moment, I got angry but could not express what I was screaming in my heart. "My faults?" "What about yours?" I cowardly swallowed his accusation too stunned to react and thought there was no other solution. Counseling did not work, we could not turn back the clock and correct the mistakes made, there was no second chance, no way to heal our marriage. Our marriage was deader than dead I thought. Later, he discussed finances with me and we agreed to divide our estate before we went to court.

Through our divorce, God has turned my life around. Many years have passed and through hindsight, I can see how God brought me through many frustrating, fearful incidents bringing me to a deeper understanding of myself and the road I chose to travel. He has been my faithful spiritual husband who loves me unconditionally and I choose to follow Him wherever He leads me.

God is all knowing and although I don't understand this side of heaven why He allows certain things to happen, I believe He has a plan for each one of us and He sees the big picture of our lives beginning to end. He just asks us to trust Him, even through tragedy. He will be faithful to see us through the good as well as the bad and will not allow anything to happen that He knows we cannot handle, He always makes a way of escape.

God allowed me to go my own way, and my life was hard. My natural instinct was to run, excuse or deny any hurtful incident especially from people I loved. Abandonment, pain and unanswered questions plagued me. I lived a nightmare not knowing or understanding the extreme emotion I felt for so many years and acted out of control trying to keep myself on an even keel. I always had to work out an end to the many incidences I found myself tangled up in instead of waiting upon the Lord and trusting Him to guide me through each day.

There are people who are crying out for help struggling with anger, emotional hurts from childhood, and or suffering pain from divorce. Let me assure you God hears you and sees your tears. In Matthew 11:28 He tells us, "Come to Me all you who are burdened and heavy laden and I will give you rest." Give God a chance to turn your life around. He is the only One who can heal your wounded heart. Every person hungers for love and acceptance. God made us that way, and He alone is the only One that can fill that hunger. He gives us joy and peace when we choose to give our lives to Him. Marriage would last a lifetime if people would fall in love with Jesus before falling in love with someone. He makes all the difference in marriage when you have a relationship with Him first.

Summing Up The Important Issues

My testimony, my story, simply written stands as proof that indeed those little traumas played subconsciously in my mind as the stress of life increased. They stunted my growth and maturity because I was unable to resolve issues where they originated. In the beginning, I stated that I could not remember most of my childhood and at first, I tried to free *myself* from repeated pain. God, I believe, saw that I was ready to accept the truth, illuminated those windows of memory to the painful experiences in my past, and helped me resolve conflicts in my spirit that were holding me back from maturing spiritually and emotionally. May you allow God to richly bless and fill you with His deep abiding love as you search and heal.

References

1 *The Source of My Strength*, Charles Stanley; Thomas Nelson Publishers, 1994

2 *Boundaries*, Henry Cloud and John Townsend; Zondervan Publishing, 1992

3 Excerpted from *Compton's Interactive Bible NIV*. Copyright (c) 1994, 1995, 1996 SoftKey Multimedia Inc. All Rights Reserved